ORTHODOX THEOLOGY

ORTHODOX THEOLOGY

An Introduction

VLADIMIR LOSSKY

Translated by
Ian and Ihita Kesarcodi-Watson

ST VLADIMIR'S SEMINARY PRESS
CRESTWOOD, NEW YORK
2001

Library of Congress Cataloging-in-Publication Data

Lossky, Vladimir, 1903-1958
Orthodox theology.

Includes bibliographical references.

1. Theology—Eastern church. 2. Theology—Doctrinal. I. Title.
BX320.2.L6713 230'.1'9 78-1853
ISBN 0-913836-43-5

ORTHODOX THEOLOGY

ST VLADIMIR'S SEMINARY PRESS
575 Scarsdale Road, Crestwood, NY 10707
1-800-204-2665

First printing 1978
Second printing 1989
Third printing 2001

ISBN 0-913836-43-5

PRINTED IN THE UNITED STATES OF AMERICA

Table of Contents

FOREWORD

It was a meeting with Leonide Ouspensky and his wife in Oxford in the mid-sixties which saw the beginnings of the translation you now have before you. The Ouspenskys and I were staying at The House of St. Sergius and St. Albans, a centre inspired, like the Society bearing the same name, by a concern for closer union between the Eastern Orthodox communion of Christendom and Anglicans.

We fell to talking of many things, among which was our mutual respect for Vladimir Lossky and his works. It was from them I learned a true communicant's interpretation of the differences in status and worth, for the *émigré* community in Paris especially, between the person and contribution of Lossky, and that other *émigré* Russian who, with Lossky, is much responsible for the vast attraction Russian Orthodoxy holds for me—Nicolas Berdyaev. Berdyaev, I was told, was mere *philosopher*, whereas Lossky was much more, namely, *theologian*. I had been an academic philosopher before going up to Oxford, and was now (that is, at that time) studying theology. I well understood this distinction. All the same, because of this *personal*, *living* expression before me, I saw in a new way much of what I had merely read in Lossky's *The Mystical Theology of the Eastern Church*, a work I still consider one of the finest expressions of authentic spirituality ever written.

The outcome of that brief encounter in a dingy room in Canterbury Road was, not one, but, to my immense delight and surprise, two items. When, in weeks hence, a superb crucifix, fashioned by Leonide's own hand, an item I still cherish as among my most valued, arrived, with it came, not only a paper or two by Leonide on "The Icon," but several back issues of the *Messager de l'Exarchat du Patriarche russe en Europe occidental* (Nos. 46, 47, 48, 49, 50 [1964-1965]), a journal distributed among the *émigré* community in Paris, carrying a series of related pieces by Lossky, under the general heading, *Théologie Dogmatique.* I eagerly read them, and there and then vowed to proffer a translation into English at the soonest propitious moment. That moment has been longer in coming than I had hoped, and it was not until some years later (1969), when I married a wife who was an expert in both French and Russian, that it was clear it was here. Even then, it was not until late 1974, on our arrival in Australia, that we actually began.

Our method has been thorough. For the French (the bulk of the script), Ihita (my wife) would make the initial translation, chapter by chapter; I would compare this translation with my own; we would discuss our differences (often the most tiresome of the stages); after agreement on these, I would rewrite the entire piece to render, not merely acceptable English sense, but also acceptable and, so far as this proved within my power, correct *theological* sense. This last stage often took *me* longer than all the others together. We would then discuss my final version and establish the shape it now has. In the case of the Russian—the Postscript, "Image and Likeness"—our method was identical, with the exception of the second stage, *my* knowledge of Russian being minimal. Ihita, on the other hand, is an expert in the language.

As a result, you have before you an English rendering of a work we consider to be of a calibre comparable to the best Lossky produced, and in sending it forth, we can only hope it has the impact on others that Lossky's other works continue to have on me.

Though I now instruct mainly in Indian spirituality, the shift in interest this may suggest away from the Orthodox tradition of Christendom may be more apparent than real. Indeed, my recent book, devoted mainly to Hinduism and titled *Eastern Spirituality* (Agam Prakashan, New Delhi, 1976), strives to illustrate its central endeavour by reference to words from Lossky's *Mystical Theology* in which he declares *his* "theological" task to be but "theos-logos"—conveying. I admit an immense debt to Lossky, and feel rather that I have moved to a different tradition of *expression* in moving the while to the Hindu and Buddhist worlds, than in any sense away from the heart of this man's teaching, or rather, "conveying." I recall Nicolas Zernov, whose illustrated lectures on "The Icon" in the Ashmolean Theatre were a highlight of my years in Oxford, in conversation confessing with a wry smile that Orthodoxy numbers the Buddha among its saints. He was referring to the famous story of Sts. Barlaam and Joasaph, a Christianized version of a Buddhist legend, in all probability the work of St. John of Damascus. Yet the broader point which he was trying to make also holds true.

Indeed, an interesting study could be done listing parallels between Lossky's expression of the Orthodox tradition and the orthodoxy of Hinduism at least. I would naturally not care to underrate the differences presented by the status of Christ in the former, but I nonetheless am ever more convinced that, in their truest *mysticisms*, much that is central to these two great traditions is largely shared. Perhaps this is true of all mysticisms, in their very nature. Perhaps there is no place more replete with Religious Knowledge, or the "wisdom" (*gnosis*, which originally comes from the Sanskrit, "*jñāna*," "sacred knowledge") it conveys, than in these traditions' varying mysticisms. The title of Lossky's main book is no accident. Nor is it an accident that Hinduism and Buddhism (also Jainism, Sikhism) sometimes are called "mystery" religions (from the Greek *mysterion*, "that which is hidden"; "hidden," that is, from merely mundane researches, being open only to what Lossky rightly styles "theology").

But here is not the place to delve further into this. I mention these parallels or possible parallels only to show why I believe there may be more to the work of this great theologian than what he presents as an apologist for just one tradition. I think there is more. I think his message is universal in a way rarely found among those normally styled "theologians" in academies purporting to study this science. For Lossky's "conveying" is in the tradition of the Cappadocian Fathers, of Dionysius the Areopagite, and of Meister Eckhart (by whom he was much influenced), a tradition which speaks to the human condition where it is now, with its *present* context and spiritual affiliations, to the human condition *here and now, shared in universally*, and not merely to some condition enjoyed only by a few of a certain tradition as paragon for the rest. I am not denying Lossky's affirmation of Christianity as in some way "superior." You merely have to look at the chapter titled "The Two Monotheisms" in this present work to note him affirming that. Nor am I suggesting that I go along with everything he says. I am merely suggesting that his *understanding* of Christianity, like that shared by the others I have mentioned, is one that already has a cosmic embrace, and already *in some way* includes all people, merely earnest in Spirit, and not one merely parochial in context. In this, he stands as a salutary corrective to many of the destructive abuses Christianity of the more parochial kind has perpetrated in its own name. In this, his works—and not least this present one—are surely crucially important in the growing world-wide yearning, signalled by such developments as the ecumenical movement within Christianity, for closer, more mutual sharing among spiritualities of different shapes and traditions.

Finally, it is well to note that a piece very similar to the appended Postscript, "Image and Likeness," has appeared as chapter six of *Mystical Theology*. Our piece, however, is rendered direct from a Russian redaction which originally appeared as "Obraz i Podobie" in *Zhurnal Moskovskoi Patriarkhii*, 3 (1958), pp. 53-64, and not from the French, as in *Mystical Theology*. There are minor differences, and these have their interest. Also, the Prologue, "Faith and Theology," originally appeared as "Foi et Theologie" in *Contacts* 13, 3-4 (1961), pp. 163-176, and not in the *Messager*. The reason for the inclusion here of these two pieces as Prologue and Postscript should be fairly clear. Apart from the chance to present the English-speaking public with two further pieces from Lossky's mature years, the latter, "Image and Likeness" ("Obraz i Podobie") anyway summarizes Lossky's "conveying" of Orthodox teaching on divine and human "shape" most splendidly, and the former, "Faith and Theology" ("Foi et Theologie"), likewise, the teaching on the place and nature of theology generally. Accordingly, the latter well concludes this presentation, and the former, quite as well begins or "sets" its ground.

I should also draw attention to the truly excellent, and, to my knowledge, exhaustive bibliography of works by Lossky found at the end of *In Image and Likeness of God*, another recent translation (1976) of selected pieces by Lossky, again from the presses of St. Vladimir's Seminary. Indeed, St. Vladimir's has in recent years published, or re-published, all of Lossky's writings presently available in English, a truly great service.

Two Codicils

A word of very special thanks in two directions. Firstly, again to the Ouspenskys, whose kind permission to proceed with this translation, not to mention the entrusting of the French form to me in the first place, has rendered the project possible. And secondly, to Mr. John H. Erickson of St. Vladimir's Seminary Press, whose encouragement and simple friendship, expressed entirely through letters, have been largely instrumental in seeing this piece to the press.

I should also add that, whilst this Foreword is the work of one hand, the translation is very clearly, and in every sense, the work of two—or rather, of four. My wife is more linguist than I, and I, more theologian than she. But together this work has been conceived; and together executed.

IAN KESARCODI-WATSON,
La Trobe University,
Victoria, Australia
1 October 1977

Prologue

FAITH AND THEOLOGY

Authentic *gnosis* is inseparable from a charisma, an illumination by grace which transforms our intelligence. And since the object of contemplation is a personal existence and presence, true gnosis implies encounter, reciprocity, *faith* as a personal adherence to the personal presence of God Who reveals Himself.

In the strict sense, among the ascetics of the Christian East gnosis constitutes the peak of the life of prayer—a peak where gnosis is *given* by God to man "who knows himself fallible," says Evagrius, and transforms his indigence in an unfolding of faith. We know Evagrius's formula, which has become an adage: "The one who has purity in prayer is true theologian, and the one who is true theologian has purity in prayer."

But purity in prayer implies the state of silence. The hesychasts are the "silents": encounter and gift, gnosis is placed beyond the νοῦς; it demands the surmounting and arrest of thought.

Accordingly, this notion of silent gnosis as true theology does not directly correspond to theological teaching, to a theology which can and must be expressed through language. The direct foundation of theological teaching is the Incarnation of the Word—just as it is for iconography. Since the Word has incarnated Himself, the Word can be thought and taught—and in the same way the Word can be painted.

But the Incarnation of the Word has no other goal than to lead us to the Father, in the Spirit. Theology as word and as thought must necessarily conceal a gnostic dimension, in the sense of the theology of contemplation and silence. It is a matter of opening our thought to a reality which goes beyond it. It is a matter of a new mode of thought where thought does not include, does not seize, but finds itself included and seized, mortified and vivified by contemplative faith. So theological teaching locates itself with difficulty between *gnosis*—charisma and silence, contemplative and existential knowledge—and *episteme*—science and reasoning.

Theological language uses *episteme*, but cannot reduce itself to it without falling yet again from this world. It must set the spirit on the path to contemplation, to pure prayer where thought stops, to the ineffable.

Indispensable to the thinking, conscientious Christian, theological teaching constitutes at once a necessity and a hindrance. Gnosis as contemplation is an exit to the state of a future age, a vision of what is beyond history, of what completes history, a projection of eschatology into the instant. Gnosis is eschatological—an unfolding of this silence which, said St. Isaac the Syrian, constitutes the language of the world which is coming.

Theological teaching, on the contrary, is made for historical work here below. It must be adopted to space and time, to environments and points in time. It must never, for all that, forget contemplation; it must fertilize itself from instants of eschatological silence and attempt to express, or at least to suggest, the ineffable. Nourished with contemplation, it does not become established in silence but seeks to speak the silence, humbly, by a new use of thought and word.

That is why theology must be praise and must dispose us to praise God. A St. Gregory of Nazianzus, a St. Simeon the New Theologian, both of whom have merited the name "Theologian," have expressed themselves with an inspired poetry. St. John of Damascus is the author of magnificent hymns that we still sing: with him theology becomes liturgical praise. Even his most scholastic statements give rise to poetic flights.

Yet theological thought can also become a hindrance, and one must avoid indulging in it, abandoning oneself to the feverish illusion of concepts. Diadochus of Photice (chaps.

67 and 68) reminds us that the intellect, until it has achieved pure prayer, finds itself confined, ill at ease, and as it were, contracted by prayer: then it prefers theological thought which allows it to "dilate" itself. But one must not forget that there is a prayer which surpasses this "dilation"—the state of those who, in all intimacy, are filled with divine grace.

Theological thought must dispose to praise and express contemplation. One must avoid it becoming a flight before the necessary "contraction" of prayer, to replace the mystery lived in silence with mental schemata easily handled, certainly, and whose use can intoxicate, but which are ultimately empty.

How, then, are we to locate taught theology with a certain fairness between the "unutterable words" heard by St. Paul in the "third heaven" (the one which goes beyond the opposition of the sensible heaven and the intelligible heaven and represents the Divine Itself, the Uncreated) and simple *episteme*, the constant temptation of the theologian? The right term could well be *sophia*, wisdom. Certainly, wisdom is a divine name. But one must take the word in its primitive sense which, in ancient Greece, indicated a certain human quality, mostly a skill, but the inspired skill of the craftsman and the artist. With Homer, *sophia,* the ἔντεχνος σοφία of the ancient Greeks, qualified the skill of the craftsman, of the artist, of the poet. The Septuagint has translated by *Sophia* the Hebrew expression which designates Divine Wisdom as God's perfect technique in His work. This sense unites with that of *economy*, of a certain prudence: *phronesis* and *sophia* are here very close.

Theology as *sophia* is connected at once to *gnosis* and to *episteme*. It reasons, but seeks always to go beyond concepts. Here a necessary moment of the *failure* of human thought breaks in before the mystery that it wants to make knowable. A theology that constitutes itself into a system is always dangerous. It imprisons in the enclosed sphere of thought the reality to which it must open thought.

In St. Paul, knowledge of God writes itself into a personal relationship expressed in terms of reciprocity: reciprocity with the object of theology (which, in reality, is a subject), reciprocity also with those to whom the theological word is addressed. At its best, it is communion: I know as I am known. Before the development of Christian theology, this mystery of communion appears absent from Greek thought: it is found only in Philo, that is to say, in a partially biblical context. Theology, then, is located in a relationship of revelation where the initiative belongs to God, while implying a human response, the free response of faith and love, which the theologians of the Reformation have often forgotten. The involvement of God calls forth our involvement. The theological quest supposes therefore the prior coming of what is quested, or rather of Him Who has already come to us and is present in us: God was the first to love us and He sent us His Son, as St. John says. This coming and this presence are seized by faith which thus underlies, with priority and in all necessity, theological thought. Certainly, faith is present in all walks, in all sciences of the human spirit, but as supposition, as working hypothesis: here, the moment of faith remains burdened with an uncertainty which proof alone could clear. Christian faith, on the contrary, is adherence to a presence which confers certitude, in such a way that certitude, here, is first. "Faith is the substance of things hoped for, the manifestation of realities unseen" (Heb. 11:1). What one quests is already present, precedes us, makes possible our questing itself. "Through faith, we comprehend (we think) how the ages have been produced" (Heb. 11:3). Thus faith allows us to think, it gives us true intelligence. Knowledge is given to us by faith, that is to say, by our participatory adherence to the presence of Him Who reveals Himself. Faith is therefore not a psychological attitude, a mere fidelity. It is an ontological relationship between man and God, an internally objective relationship for which the catechumen prepares himself, and through which baptism and chrismation are conferred upon the faithful: gifts which restore and vivify the deepest nature of man. "In baptism," said Irenaeus, "one receives the immutable canon of truth." It is first the "rule of faith," transmitted to the initiated. But this *regula fidei* (Tertullian,

Irenaeus) implies the very faculty of receiving it. "The heretics who have perverted the rule of truth," St. Irenaeus wrote, "preach themselves when they believe that they are preaching Christianity (*Adversus haereses*, Book III). This faculty is the personal existence of man, it is his nature made to assimilate itself to divine life—both mortified in their state of separation and death and vivified by the presence of the Holy Spirit. Faith as ontological participation included in a personal meeting is therefore the first condition for theological knowledge.

Theology as *sophia* would therefore be the capacity, the skill to adapt one's thought to revelation, to find skillful and inspired words which would bear witness in the language—but not in the limits—of human thought, in replying to the needs of the moment. It is a matter of the internal reconstruction of our faculties of knowing, conditioned by the presence in us of the Holy Spirit. "You have received the anointing of the Holy One and you all know . . . The anointing you have received from Him remains in you and you have no need to be taught. And as His anointing teaches you about everything... as it has taught you, abide Him" (I John 2:20, 27). The anointing—*chrism*—denotes here the presence of the Holy Spirit: Christians are the anointed, the Christs of the Lord. Nobody therefore can teach us the truth if this presence, which opens to us all knowledge, is not already within us. It is a true Christian transposition of the Platonic *anamnesis*, since the *chrism* gives us knowledge of all things: the Christian knows all, but theology is necessary to actuate this knowledge. Already in the Prophets, particularly in Jeremiah, one finds the notion of this knowledge which will be given to all men by the Spirit of God: "I shall place My law in the depths of their being and I shall write it on their hearts.... They shall all know Me..." (Jer. 31:33-34).

Outside of faith, theology has no sense: it can only be based on interior evidence of the truth in the Spirit, on the teaching of the truth by the truth itself. The *regula fidei* is the first actuation of this evidence. It is this interior evidence that is stressed by St. Augustine in his treatise on the *Interior*

Master: I have spoken to all. However, those in whom anointing does not speak, those who are not taught inwardly by the Holy Spirit always departed *indocti*. "The flesh of Him Who teaches is found in the heavens: I speak of the Lord...." "Only the action of Christ in the heart allows the heart not to remain in solitude. Only the Interior Master teaches. Where His anointing is absent, external words assail the ears to no purpose."

No one can therefore assume the exclusive right of teaching in the Church. The Spirit is given to all, anointing the Master alone, the Christ. The Spirit which inspires him who teaches must be found in those who listen, else they will hear nothing. They will therefore be not only listeners but judges. Each must become witness to the truth. The sense of external teaching is to actuate the gift of the Spirit so that our thought also participates in faith. Faith must be aware, it must actuate, with an existential consciousness, the "substance of things hoped for," their presence in us. Faith mortifies and vivifies the intellect, it makes the intelligence bear fruit through an altogether new ontological relationship with God, a relationship proper to the Christian and which is the criterion within us of truth.

God speaks to us through His Son, the Incarnation accomplishes revelation: it reveals and it constitutes revelation itself. To think theologically is not to think of this revelation, but to think by means of it. The Fathers often invoke "our philosophy." In fact, the method of this "philosophy" (which properly denotes theology) is based on an approach opposite to that of speculation. Theology starts from a fact: revelation. "God has spoken to us finally through His Son" (Heb. 1:2). The philosophy which speculates on God starts, on the contrary, from an idea. For the theologian, the point of departure is Christ, and it is also the point of arrival. The philosopher raises himself to an idea from another idea or from a group of generalized facts according to an idea. For certain philosophers, the search for God corresponds to an inherent necessity in their thought: God must exist so that their conception of the universe might be coherent. There follows the search for arguments to demonstrate the existence of this necessary God—whence these "proofs of the existence of God," "proofs" which the theologian can well do without.

It is therefore not surprising that the notion of the absolute should be very different according to the philosophers. The God of Descartes is a mathematician's God: to justify the innate ideas of mathematical truths, a supreme mathematician who has calculated everything in all eternity is necessary. It is by the will of such a God that two parallel lines can never cross. For Leibnitz, God is necessary to justify the pre-established harmony between our perception and reality. For each person constitutes a closed world. Hence, that all these worlds may correspond, that they may form but a single one, there must be a supreme Monad in which the monads converge and order themselves harmoniously, in such a way that the truth of perception for one coincides with that of perception for all. Only God, it has been said, could write the Monadology. Kant's entire thought questions metaphysics: we know only our perceptions, and Kant, to explain the possibility of knowledge, does an analysis of its conditions. But he needs the idea of God in the moral sphere: for him, in his *Critique of Practical Reason*, God appears as the necessary postulate of moral life. In his private life, Kant was a professing and practising Lutheran. In his metaphysics, he refuses all speculation upon God. But, in his ethics, he postulates God's existence. The God of Bergson is a God of creative evolution. It is the vital impulse, an absolute in becoming.

It is more difficult to discover God as the intellectual keystone in the philosophies of antiquity. Even here, nonetheless, the God of Aristotle is the unmoved mover postulated by the existence of movement. He is also, in his speculation on being, primary substance—thought which thinks itself and moves itself, the pure intellectual act. Plato never speaks—or almost never—of God. However, it was necessary for him to give foundation to a certain very concrete idea: the possibility of a just man, of a sage. Socrates was condemned by the city because he practised a different justice, the true one. How then was one to justify true justice, how to construct a State where the just man had his place? Raising himself thus from this fundamental demand towards the knowledge of that which really is, Plato discovers stable reality in the world of ideas which thought alone can grasp. Going even higher, he has a presentiment of the "Good which is beyond being" (the seventh book of *The Republic*): when he reaches this point, he forgets the search for a just State, and justice itself, in contemplation. The point of departure and the point of arrival, nevertheless, remain human. *The Republic* concludes with the necessity of giving power to philosophers, or rather of obliging them to govern, at least for a certain time, for those who know beatitude do not wish to descend again into the cave.

Theological procedure is quite different. Since God reveals Himself to us, our whole thought—really, our whole approach, our *conversatio*—should respond and correspond to this fact, should conform to this revelation gathered in faith. Philosophers construct an idea of God. For the theologian, God is someone Who reveals Himself and Who cannot be known outside of revelation. One must open oneself to this personal God, to encounter Him in a total involvement: that is the only way to know Him. But this concrete and personal God contains the abstract and impersonal God of philosophers Who is not, most often, a mere mirage, but also a reflection in human thought of the personal God. Certainly, starting from this reflection, by reflection or by speculation, it is impossible to know the real God. The procedure of faith is necessary, fundamental, primordial. But then this God of the philosophers takes His place in the total reality of the living God: as Clement of Alexandria wrote, "He will grow unto the plenitude of Christ." Christ is the perfect measure of all things: He breaks the closed systems in which the philosophers imprison and denature the reflection of the living God in human thought—but He also brings His accomplishment to the intuitive attention which the philosophers have devoted to this reflection.

Nevertheless, one cannot make from these intuitions, from these thoughts, an introduction to theology: that would be to reverse the correct relationship. One has no right to start from a treatise *De deo uno*, from a God Who is a purely intellectual substance accessible to reason, possessing all perfections to an eminent degree, containing all ideas of all things, principle of every order and every reality. For then, to go from this God to the Trinity, one must juxtapose—for reasons of credibility, it will be said—the God of revelation with that of the philosophers. Now, in producing these reasons, one remains on the level of "natural theology," one continues to play the philosophers' game. A Christian has no right to separate, even in thought, the One and the Three when he speaks of God. To go, rationally so to speak, from the One to the Three, is a *tour de force*, an intellectual conjuring trick rather than a logical development.

One must therefore start from faith—and that is the only way to save philosophy. Philosophy itself, on its summits, demands the renunciation of speculation; questing God, it attains the moment of supreme ignorance: a negative way where the failure of human thought is acknowledged. Here, philosophy ends in a mysticism and dies in becoming the experience of an Unknown God Who can no longer even be named. It is this Unknown God that St. Paul came to preach (to the court) upon the Areopagus. In fact, we know that the altar to the Unknown God was erected in honour of one of the many gods whom one was afraid of ignoring or disregarding, Athens being a mighty mother-city. Paul, nevertheless, seems to have known the best of Greek thought, Stoicism for example, and it is to the best of this thought that he wished to reply.

If the summit of philosophy is a question, theology must reply by bearing witness that transcendence is revealed in the immanence of the Incarnation. The notion of revelation implies this immanence. But, in this immanence itself, God reveals Himself as transcendent. To evoke transcendence seriously in a Christian perspective, one must go beyond not only all the notions of the created world, but also the notion of the first cause of this world. Divine causality in the creation supposes yet again a link with its effect. God must be conceived beyond philosophical transcendence: one must transcend the transcendence of this first causality which puts

God in relation with the world. One must admit that the world has been created freely by God, but that God might just as well not have created it. Creation is a free act of divine will. In the great Platonic tradition, God is always conceived as the principle of everything that exists and the world develops from them, without ontological break. For Christians, on the contrary, all emanationism is impossible, the ontological break is total, creation *ex nihilo* is free. Here is a proper—and fundamental—given of the biblical tradition, whether Judaeo-Christian or Abrahamic.

The world would not have existed were God not even that which He is. In Exodus, God calls Himself: "I am He Who is." Christians have wanted to see in this divine name the response to all human philosophies. They have justified the philosophers by reading this passage. The being that one cannot name names Himself. This Name above all is independent of every other existence. It will subsist after the destruction of the universe—"separated" from all being—and will ontologically restore the universe, as the rabbinical tradition says. It is the name of "Him Who is" in an absolute manner. In his *Confessions* (Book 7), St. Augustine evokes his meditation on this text: "Thou didst call me from afar, saying: In truth, *ego sum qui sum.* And I heard Thee as one hears in the heart, and I could no longer doubt. I could have doubted more easily the fact that I was alive than that the truth exists"—truth which can be known in contemplating creation: beings really do not have being, "they are because they are from Thee, they are not because they are not what Thou art."

This name—at least, such as understood by St. Augustine and many of the Fathers: God as plenitude of being—still remains, however, on the conceptual sphere. We conceive being by starting from what we know as being from beings. It is not a really "separated" name. One must evoke God beyond all that can be known as being. As Hegel has shown, the concept of being is opposed to that of non-being; being and nothingness, while constituting two concept-limits, remain linked. God, the living God, is beyond this supreme conceptual couple. Hegel's critique stresses that being is the most vacuous of notions, the most abstract and impoverished of concepts, virtually identical to its opposite, non-being. The notion of being is, in sum, our thought becoming its own object. Concrete beings exist concretely. The concept of being is none other than our thought about them, what is abstractly common to them. One knows Hegel's solution: to find reality, one must think being and non-being together, think them together as movement, as concrete becoming; Hegel's God is divinized dialectic. Becoming appears as the first concrete concept.

Let us remember only that the concept of "being" cannot denote the highest but only the lowliest. The living God must be evoked beyond the opposition of being and non-being, beyond all concepts, including, of course, that of becoming. He cannot be opposed to anything. He knows no nothingness which would oppose Him. Thought must go beyond itself to approach Him—without naming Him. One must grasp Him by not grasping, know Him by not knowing. Such is the only natural theology for a Christian. "*Attingitur inattingibile inattingibiliter,*" said Nicholas of Cusa, in a compact formula that may be translated thus: "That which is beyond all attainment cannot be attained except in a manner which does not attain it." One cannot fix God with a concept, even that of essence. Such is "learned ignorance."

God therefore remains transcendent, radically transcendent by His nature, in the very immanence of His manifestation. That is why the apophatic (or negative) way has been adopted by Christians, finding its perfect expression in the Pseudo-Areopagite who wrote his *Mystical Theology* towards the end of the fifth century. The apophatic way, in the Dionysian sense, demands in speaking of God the negation of the highest names; even the One of Plotinus does not suit this God Who transcends every human notion. One would find the same attitude in St. Augustine: "God is He Whom we know best in not knowing Him." It is He about Whom we have no knowledge unless it be to know how we do not know Him (*De ordine*). And in his *De doctrina christiana*, Augustine stresses that one cannot even say that

God is ineffable, since by saying this we say something and raise a "battle of words" which must be overcome by silence.

Thus is demonstrated the breakdown of human thought before the radical transcendence of God. Philosophy took itself as far as this breakdown in the great Platonic line. Plato, in the *Phaedo* and in *The Republic* (Book 6, 19. 529b) evokes "the Beautiful which surpasses all possibility of expression." In the *Parmenides* is found the first hypothesis about the One: if the One is really one, It is not being, since the thought of being implies a dyad, that of being and non-being. We can have no opinion, thought, or knowledge of It; It is beyond everything. Dionysius was to cite this text literally—what is more, without naming Plato. Finally, it is well known that Plotinus elaborated this negative way most remarkably.

On revelation, the First Epistle of John states: "No one has ever seen God" (I John 4:12). And St. Paul says: "God alone possesses immortality. He resides in inaccessible light; no man has seen Him or can see Him" (I Tim. 6:16).

One must understand that the apophasis of Eastern theology is not borrowed from the philosophers. The God of the Christians is more transcendent than that of the philosophers. In Plotinus, the One, the Absolute that cannot be named, is in a certain manner in continuity with the Intellect, and finally with the world. The universe appears as a manifestation, as a degradation of the Absolute—moreover, without any catastrophic process. One must remember Plotinus' aversion for the gnostics. Cosmogony coincides with theogony. For Christians, on the contrary, the break is radical between the living God—the Trinity—and the created world, as much in its intelligible modality as in its sensible modality. The Fathers have used the philosophical technique of negation in order to posit the transcendence, absolute this time, of the living God. The apophaticism of Orthodox theology is no technique of interiorization whereby one absorbs oneself into an absolute more or less "co-natural" with the Intellect. It is a prostration before the living God, radically ungraspable, unobjectifiable and unknowable, because He is personal, because He is the free plenitude of personal existence. *Apophasis is the inscription in human language, in theological language, of the mystery of faith.* For this unknowable God reveals Himself, and, because He transcends, in His free personal existence, His very essence, He can really make Himself a participator. "No one has ever seen God: His only Son, He Who is in the bosom of the Father has manifested Him to us" (John 1:18). This mystery of faith as personal encounter and ontological participation is the unique foundation of theological language, a language that apophasis opens to the silence of deification.

Chapter One

THE TWO MONOTHEISMS

I. Introduction

God is not the object of a science, and theology differs radically from the thought of philosophers. The theologian does not search for God as a man seeks an object; he is seized by Him as one is seized by a person. And it is because he has initially been found by God, because God, one might say, has gone forth to find him in the encounter of revelation, that he can then search for God, as one searches for a presence with all one's being (and so also with one's intellect). The God of theology is a "Thou"; He is the living God of the Bible, the Absolute, certainly, but a personal Absolute whom one can address intimately in prayer.

The relationship of "I-Thou" between a devotee and a personal God is, of course, also encountered outside of the Judaeo-Christian tradition. But this god is not then the supreme and unique God; he is only one of the numerous divine personages of a polytheism. Polytheism is in general only the lesser aspect of a monotheism; but the absolute into which the "gods" reabsorb themselves is never personal. The "gods"—and, in India, even the "personal" god—are no more than aspects, manifestations of an impersonal absolute: manifestations as contingent, for the non-Christian Orient, as the world which they confront, being destined like it to efface themselves, to absorb themselves in the inwardness of Total Identity. And this Identity ignores "the other," engulfing all personal relationship.

Similarly in the religion of ancient Greece, the gods had to submit to an anonymous and dominating "Necessity." The philosophers placed above these gods, not a Person, but a superior universe of stability and light, the sphere of beauty of an impersonal being—thus Plato, the Stoics and even Aristotle. And "Neo-Platonism" was to end in a "mysticism" of absorption which reminds us of India.

It is worth pausing a while on Plotinus, who represents perhaps the peak of non-biblical antiquity, and whose thought will be assimilated and used by numerous Fathers, attaining through them a true fulfillment.

For Plotinus, the first level of knowledge is located in the *World-Soul*, which integrates the diverse unity of the cosmos, and of which the gods are so many aspects. Above this—in man as at the heart of the world—is *Intelligence*, an even higher degree of unity. This level of νοῦς is also that of being, or rather, there is an identity between νοῦς and being, between thought and its object; the object exists because it is thought, the thought, because the object finally reduces to an intellectual essence. This identity, however, is not absolute, since it transposes itself into an alternating reciprocity in which otherness still subsists. To know the One fully it is, then, necessary to transcend νοῦς.

When one goes beyond the thought and the thought reality, the ultimate dyad of Being and Intelligence, one arrives at non-Intelligence and non-Being, the negation here indicating something positive, a transcendence. But then silence imposes itself: one cannot name the ineffable, since it opposes itself to nothing, since nothing limits it. The only way to attain it is through not knowing it: the non-knowledge, a breaking-through beyond everything, which is ecstasy. Philosophy culminates and suicides at the threshold of the unknowable. One can only know the One before and after the ecstasy; that is to say one cannot know it since it is not the ecstasy. And during the latter, there is no longer anything else, hence no knowing. Four times in his life, Porphyry tells us, Plotinus knew ecstasy. But this knowledge of divine nature is achieved and canceled out simultaneously in the impersonality of unknowing.

Against the majority of religions and metaphysics where the relationship "I-Thou" disappears as soon as one ventures into the sphere proper to divinity, the Bible affirms the irreducible ultimacy of a personal God, at once absolute and personal. But then, in connection with the full revelation of Christianity, another limitation emerges: the God of the Jews hides the profundities of His nature; He manifests Himself only through His authority; His name itself is unpronounceable. He surrounds Himself with inaccessible light and man cannot see Him without dying: neither true reciprocity nor face to face encounter are possible between this terrifying divine monad and the humility of the created. From God alone comes speech, Word; from man comes only the obscurity of obedience and of faith. "Theology," in the proper sense, as it is understood by the Fathers, remains closed to Israel.

Thus outside of Christianity one sees these oppositions: among the Jews (and later in Islam, which is "Abrahamic") a monotheism which affirms the personal character of God but is ignorant of His nature, a living God but not the divine life; in the ancient world (and still today in traditions alien to the Semitic) a metaphysical monotheism which anticipates the nature of the Absolute but can only gain access to it by dissolving the person. On one hand one finds a personal mysticism of absorption where knowledge of God proves impossible, since His person itself must be reabsorbed into the ineffable; on the other, a personal obedience to a personal God but without a vision of the divine nature, a knowledge forbidden by the person of God since this is closed upon itself: on one side, nature drowning the person, on the other side the divine person hiding nature. Thus, outside of Christianity an impossible knowledge (since it denies the known and the knower) and a forbidden knowledge (since there is no common measure, no mediation, between the Creator and the creature) are opposed.

Christianity frees man from these two limitations, by revealing fully and at once the personal God and His nature. It thus accomplishes the best of Israel and the best of the other religions or metaphysics, not as a cultural synthesis, but in Christ and through Christ. In Him, indeed, humanity and divinity are united, and divine nature communicates itself to human nature to deify it: this is the answer to Israel. But the Son is consubstantial with the Father and with the Spirit; and this is the answer to impersonal metaphysics. The divine nature is not beyond the person: its fullness, on the contrary, resides in the communion of the divine persons, and its communication to man is effected by a personal communion.

But these answers are difficult to understand, and this fulfillment in Christ is both "scandal" and "folly":

— "scandal to the Jews": how could the unique, the transcendent, the God without common measure with man, have a Son, Himself God, and yet a man, humiliated and crucified?

— "folly to the Greeks": how could the impersonal Absolute incarnate itself in a person, how could unmoving eternity enter into time? How could God become that which one must, necessarily, go beyond to merge with Him?

Thus Christianity at once fulfills and scandalizes. But whatever may be the attitude of the "Greeks" and the "Jews" who deny Christ, in the Church—that is to say in the body of this Word which reclaims all things, makes anew, purifies and puts every truth in its proper place—there should be no difference between Greek and Jew.

Two dangers appear here: the first is that the theologian may be a "Greek" in the Church, that he may allow himself to be dominated by his forms of expression to the point of intellectualizing revelation, and to lose at once the biblical sense of the concrete and this existential character of the encounter with God which is concealed in the apparent anthropomorphism of Israel. To this danger, which goes from the Scholastics to the intellectuals of the nineteenth century, corresponds in our age an inverse danger: that of a somewhat "structured" biblicism which wishes to oppose the Hebrew tradition to "Greek philosophy," and attempts to remake theory in purely Semitic categories.

But theology must be of universal expression. It is not by accident that God has placed the Fathers of the Church in a Greek setting; the demands for lucidity in philosophy and profundity in gnosis have forced them to purify and to sanctify the language of the philosophers and of the mystics, to give to the Christian message, which includes but goes beyond Israel, all its universal reach.

II. The Negative and the Positive Way

God is known in revelation as in a personal relationship. Revelation is always revelation to someone; it is made up of encounters which order themselves into a history. Revelation in its totality is therefore a history; it is the reality of history, from creation to the parousia.

Revelation is thus a "theocosmic" relationship which includes us. Not only can we not know God outside it, but we cannot judge it "objectively" from outside. Revelation knows of no "outside," for it *is* this relationship between God and the world within which, like it or not, we find ourselves.

But in the immanence of revelation, God affirms Himself to be transcendent to creation. If one were to define as transcendent that which escapes the sphere of our knowledge and experience, one must say that God not only is not a part of this world but even transcends His own revelation.

God is immanent and transcendent at the same time: immanence and transcendence mutually imply one another. Pure transcendence is impossible: if one conceives God as the transcendent cause of the universe, He cannot be purely transcendent since the very idea of a cause implies that of effect. In the dialectic of revelation, immanence allows us to name transcendence. But there would be no immanence whatsoever if transcendence were not, in its depth, inaccessible.

That is why we cannot think of God in Himself, in His essence, in His secrecy. To attempt to think of God in Himself reduces us to silence, as neither thought nor language can imprison the infinite in those concepts which, in defining, limit. That is why the Greek Fathers had recourse, for knowledge of God, to *the negative way.*

The negative (apophatic) way attempts to know God not in what He is (that is to say, in relation to our experience as creatures) but in what He is not. It proceeds by a series of negations. The Neo-Platonists and India use this way too, as it is imposed on all thought which turns to God, raising itself towards Him. It culminates, with Plotinus, in the suicide of philosophy, in the metamorphosis of the philosopher into the mystic. But outside of Christianity, it only ends in the depersonalization of God, and of the man who seeks Him. Thus an abyss separates this quest from Christian theology, even when the latter appears to follow the way of Plotinus. Indeed, a Gregory of Nyssa or a Pseudo-Dionysius the Areopagite (in his treatise, *On Mystical Theology*) does not see, in apophaticism, revelation but the receptacle of revelation: they arrive at the personal presence of a hidden God. For them the negative way is not resolved in a void where subject and object will be reabsorbed; the human person is not dissolved but has access to a face to face encounter with God, a union without confusion according to grace.

Apophaticism consists in negating that which God is not; one eliminates firstly all creation, even the cosmic glory of the starry heavens and the intelligible light of the angels in the sky. Then one excludes the most lofty attributes, goodness, love, wisdom. One finally excludes being itself. God is none of all this; in His own nature He is the unknowable. He "is not." But here is the Christian paradox; He is the God to Whom I say "Thou," Who calls me, Who reveals Himself as personal, as living. In the liturgy of St. John Chrysostom, before the Lord's Prayer, one prays: "And grant us, O Lord, to dare to invoke Thee with confidence and without fear, by calling Thee Father." The Greek text says exactly this: "Thou, ἐπουράνιον Θεὸν (*i.e.* God on high Whom one cannot name, the apophatic God), to name Thee Father and to dare to invoke Thee." One prays to have the audacity and the simplicity to say "Thou" to God.

Thus, side by side with the negative way, the positive way, "cataphatic," opens out. God Who is the hidden God, beyond all that reveals Him, is also He that reveals Himself.

He is wisdom, love, goodness. But His nature remains unknowable in its depths, and that is exactly why He reveals Himself. The permanent memory of apophaticism must rectify the cataphatic way. It must purify our concepts by contact with the inaccessible, and prevent them from being enclosed within their limited meanings. Certainly God is wise, but not in the banal sense of a merchant or a philosopher. And His limitless wisdom is not an internal necessity of His nature. The highest names, even love, express but do not exhaust the divine essence. They constitute the attributes by which divinity communicates itself without its secret source, its nature, ever becoming exhausted, or becoming objectified beneath our scrutiny. Our purified concepts enable us to approach God; the divine names enable us in some sense even to enter into Him. But we can never seize His essence, else He would be determined by His attributes; but He is determined by nothing and that is precisely why He is personal.

St. Gregory of Nyssa has commented in this sense upon the Song of Songs, in which he sees the mystical marriage of the soul (and the Church) with God. The lover who pursues the beloved is the soul seeking its God. The beloved rises and escapes, God does the same: the more the soul knows Him, the more He escapes, and the more it loves Him. The more God satisfies it with His presence, the more it thirsts for a presence which is more total, and rushes headlong in pursuit. The more it is filled with God, the more it discovers Him transcendent. Thus the soul is penetrated with the divine presence, but sinks ever deeper into the inexhaustible essence, inaccessible in as much as it is essence. Thus this pursuit becomes unending, and in this infinite dilation of the soul where love unceasingly overflows and renews itself from "beginning to beginning," Gregory sees the Christian notion of beatitude. If one knew the very nature of God, one would be God. The union of the creature with the Creator is this limitless flight where the soul, the more it is fulfilled, fortunately perceives this distance increasingly shortened but always infinite between itself and the divine essence, a distance which allows and calls forth love. God calls us and we are included in this call which reveals Him and conceals Him at the same time; and we cannot reach Him unless it be in this relationship which, to exist, demands that in His essence God remains forever out of reach.

The Old Testament itself knows this negative moment; this is the image, so often used by the Christian contemplatives, of darkness. "He has made darkness His abode," chants Psalm 17, and Solomon, in his prayer of consecration of the Temple (Book of Kings) says to God: "Thou Who hast wished to dwell in darkness." Let us think also of the darkness of Sinai.

The experience of this transcendence is appropriate to the mystical life of the Christian: "Even when I am united unto Thee," says St. Macarius, "even when it seems to me that I no longer am separate from Thee, I know that Thou art the master and I the servant." This is no longer the ineffable fusion of the ecstasy of Plotinus, but a personal relationship which, far from diminishing the Absolute, reveals it to be "other," that is to say, always new, inexhaustible. This is the relationship between the person of God, a nature as such inaccessible (the idea of essence here does not bar love—on the contrary—but represents the logical impossibility of a "voyage to the limit," which would surround and exhaust God), and the person of man, man even in his nothingness, as a person who, in the union, does not become abolished but is transfigured and remains, or rather fully becomes, a person. Otherwise there is no longer *religio*, that is to say, a bond, a relationship.

The source of true Christian theology is thus the confession of the Incarnation of the Son of God. Through the Incarnation, indeed, a person unites in himself the transcendent, unknowable nature of divinity, to human nature. The union of the two natures in Christ is that of the supracelestial and the earthly, carried as far as the tomb, as far, indeed, as Hell. In Christ transcendence is made immanent and gives us the possibility of talking about God, that is, of being theologians. Here lies all the mystery, that man may see (and sees) God in Christ, that he may see (and sees) in Christ the shining forth of the divine nature. This union without mixture of divinity and humanity in a single person excludes a metaphysical apophasis which would sweep away the Trinity to engulf itself in the impersonal: on the contrary, it manages to establish revelation as an encounter, a communion.

Thus Greek thought has at once opened and closed the way to Christianity. It opened it by celebrating the Logos and the celestial beauty, if not of God, at least of the divine. It closed it by thrusting the wise man back towards a salvation through evasion . Some have wished to oppose the *joie de vivre* of the ancient world to the sombre character of Christianity. This is to forget the tragic sense of destiny in the Greek theatre, and the sharp ascetism of Plato, his equation "body=tomb" (σῶμα=σῆμα), the dualism which he introduced between the sensible and the intelligible, to disqualify at once the sensible, simple reflection, and to invite one to flee from it. In a certain way, ancient thought prepares the way not only for Christianity, where it is superseded, but also for the more or less crude dualisms of the gnostic systems and Manichaeism, where it is set against Christ.

That which is lacking in this thought, that which would be at once a chance of fulfillment and a stumbling-block for it, is the reality of the Incarnation. St. Augustine, when he remembers his youth, is the admirable witness of this confrontation between Antiquity and Christianity: "There I have read," he says, in recalling his discovery of the *Enneads*, "that in the beginning was the Word (*i.e.* he rediscovers St. John in Plotinus). I have read that the human soul lends witness to the light, but is not itself light. . . . But I have certainly not found that the Word came to this world and was not received there. I have not found that the Word became flesh. I have found that the Son can be the equal of the Father, but not that He annihilated Himself, humiliated unto death on the Cross . . . and that God the Father gave Him the name of Jesus." It is, on the contrary, with this very name that theology starts.

III. The Trinity

The Incarnation, the point of departure for theology, immediately puts at the heart of the latter the mystery of the Trinity. He Who is incarnated is indeed none other than the Word, that is to say, the second person of the Trinity. Incarnation and Trinity are thus inseparable, and against a certain Protestant criticism, against a liberalism which would oppose Gospel and theology, we must stress the evangelical roots of the orthodox triadology. Can one indeed read the Gospel without asking the question: who is Jesus? And when we hear the confession of Peter: "Thou art the Son of the living God" (Matt. 16:16), when St. John opens to us eternity with his Gospel, we understand that the only possible answer is the dogma of the Trinity, the Christ, only Son of the Father, God equal to the Father, identical divinity and different person.

The chief source of our knowledge of the Trinity is, indeed, none other than the Prologue of St. John (and also the first epistle of the same), and that is why the author of these amazing texts has received, in the Orthodox tradition the name of St. John the Theologian. From the first verse of the Prologue, the Father is called God, Christ is called the Word—and the Word, in this beginning which is here not temporal but ontological, is at once God ("in the beginning . . . the Word was God") and other than the Father ("and the Word was with God"). These three affirmations of St. John: "In the beginning was the Word—and the Word was with God—and the Word was God," constitute the germ of all trinitarian theology. They immediately direct our thought to the obligation of affirming, at the same time, the identity and the diversity of God.

Certainly it is tempting to shatter the antinomy by rationalizing one or the other of its terms. Thus there have appeared, more or less explicitly, two major heretical tendencies: Unitarianism and Tritheism.

Unitarianism has often assumed the aspect of an absolute monarchianism: there is only one person in God, that of the Father, Whose Son and Spirit are only emanations or forces. Its most perfect expression was in the third century, the modalism of Sabellius, where the very notion of personhood disappeared. For Sabellius indeed, God is an impersonal essence which manifests itself diversely to the universe. The three persons are then no longer anything but three successive modes of action, three appearances to the world of the same monad always simple in itself. Through creation God takes on the shape of Father. The Father is thus the aspect of a first phase of divine manifestation linked with the genesis and the paradisiacal state. But sin modified the relation between God and man; the era of the Father finished and God took another aspect, that of the Son, whose complete manifestation corresponded to the Incarnation. With the Ascension, the filial mode of divinity was once more absorbed into the essential indistinction and a new mode appeared, that of the Spirit. At the Final Judgement, when the universe will be divinized, everything will enter into the indivisible monad. This successive Trinity remains thus a pure appearance and in no way concerns the reality itself of God: here, nature completely absorbs the persons.

The opposite heresy, pure Tritheism, has never been expressed. But if the absurdity of a divergent Trinity cannot be formulated, one often observes a certain weakening of the trinitarian reciprocity: a Trinity without equality and finally relinquished. Before Nicaea subordinationistic tendencies were powerful in Christian thought, particularly with Origen. Under the influence of Neo-Platonism, the Father was identified with supreme unity, so that one could not thereafter distinguished the Son except by subordinating Him. Divinity did not properly belong to Him; He only participated in the divine nature of the Father. The Logos thus became the instrument of the One, and the Holy Spirit in its turn served as an instrument for the Son with which to sanctify on behalf of the Father.

With Arius this tendency became a heresy which broke the trinitarian unity. Arius identified God and the Father, and claimed that all which is not God is created. The Son is therefore created, since He is other than the Father, and the personal difference results in an ontological break. This created Son creates in His turn the Spirit, and the Trinity reverts to a hierarchy where the inferior serves as instrument to the superior, and which is shot clean through by that insuperable gap which separates the created from the uncreated. Generation becomes creation, the Son and the Spirit, "grandsons," who are creatures radically distinct from paternal divinity, and the triad only survives by dividing the monad.

By contrast, faith, jealously preserved by the Church, seizes in a single movement, with a single adhesion, the unity and the diversity of God. But our intelligence must also be religious, and it is not only feeling, but also thought, which must open itself to the truth, or rather neither of them separately but our whole being, at once fervent and lucid. The triumph of Christian thought is to have elaborated over the first four centuries, and particularly during the fourth, "trinitarian" *par excellence,* a definition which gave to the heathen an inkling of the fullness of the Trinity: this was not the rationalization of Christianity but the Christianization of reason, a transmuting of philosophy into contemplation, a saturation of thought by a mystery which is not a secret to conceal, but an inexhaustible light. This grand work, over which Athanasius of Alexandria, Basil, Gregory of Nyssa and Gregory of Nazianzus, and also Hilary of Poitiers, all collaborated, finally enabled the Church to express, by the term ὁμοούσιος, the mystery of the divinity at once monad and triad. Ὁμοούσιος means consubstantial, identical in essence, co-essential; this is the adjective which qualifies the Son, God and other than "*the* God," the same but not the Father.

"The Word was with God" says the Prologue of St. John: πρὸς τὸν Θεόν. Πρὸς denotes movement, a dynamic closeness: one could translate it as "towards" rather than "with": "The Word was *towards* God." Πρὸς thus includes the idea of a relationship: this relationship between the Father and the Son is eternal generation, and we are thus introduced, by the Gospel itself, to the life of the divine persons of the Trinity.

It is also the Gospel that reveals to us the trinitarian

"location" of the Holy Spirit, and the relations which stress Its own personal uniqueness. It is enough to read in St. John the last words of the Lord to the Apostles: "And I will pray to the Father to send you another Comforter (Protector) to be with you always: . . . the Spirit of Truth" (15:16-17) and again: "The Protector, the Holy Spirit Whom the Father will send in my Name" (15:26). The Spirit is then other than the Son, Who is also a Comforter, but He, the Spirit, is sent in the name of the Son to bear witness to Him. His relation to the Son is then neither one of opposition nor of separation, but of diversity and reciprocity—thus, of communion in the Father.

It is the same for the relation of the Spirit to the Father: "The Spirit of Truth which proceeds from the Father" (15:26): the Spirit is different from the Father, but united to Him by a bond of procession which is proper to Him and differs from the generation of the Son.

The Son and the Spirit thus appear, throughout the Gospel, as two divine persons sent into the world, the former to quicken our personal liberty, the latter to unite Itself with our nature and regenerate it. These two persons each have their proper relation to the Father (generation and procession); they also have between them a relationship of reciprocity: it is thanks to the purification of the Virgin by the Spirit that the Son could be given to men, as it is by the prayer of the Son ascended back to the right hand of the Father that the Spirit is dispensed to them ("the Protector Whom I will send you from the Father," John 15:26). And these two persons appear, in the eternity which unfolds, equal in dignity to the Father and identical to Him in substance. They transcend the world where they act: the one and the other are indeed "with" the Father, Who does not Himself come into the world, and their closeness to the Father, source of the divine nature, manages to locate for our thought the Trinity in its transcendence, its stability and its fullness.

IV. Trinitarian Terminology

The great problem of the fourth century was to express at once divine unity and diversity, the coincidence in God of the monad and the triad. One is then present, with the Fathers, at a true transmutation of language: using either philosophical terms or words of the current language, they change their meaning until they are rendered able to encompass this prodigiously new reality which Christianity alone reveals: namely, that of personhood—in God as in man, since man is in the image of God; and in the Trinity as in regenerated humanity, since the Church reflects the divine life.

To express the reality common to the three, "dividing in three the non-divisible divinity," as Gregory of Nazianzus says, the Fathers chose the word οὐσία. This word belonged to the language of philosophy and meant "essence," though it was soon vulgarized to mean, for example, a "property" or a "category." It had an ontological resonance, derived as it is from the verb εἰμί, "to be," and could be well used to stress the ontological unity of divinity, especially as one also finds it in the term ὁμοούσιος, already Christianized by the council of Nicaea, to denote the co-essentiality of the Father and the Son. Ὁμοούσιος and οὐσία, however, insisted on identity, and this was the familiar road to the thought of late Hellenism, centred, as we have said, on the ecstatic discovery of the One. Ὁμοούσιος had already introduced an immense innovation, since the identity of essence which it expressed unified, without reabsorbing them into their own unity, two irreducibly different persons. But it was precisely this, the mystery of "the other," that had to be affirmed, being on this occasion so radically foreign to the thought of the ancients, who tended, ontologically, to put a high value upon "sameness," and to denounce in the notion of "the other" what they took to be a disintegration of being. Significant of this attitude in the vocabulary of the ancients was the absence of any designation for "person." For the Latin *persona,* the Greek πρόσωπον merely denoted the delimiting, deceptive, and finally illusory aspect of the individual: not the open-face of personal being, but the masked-face of impersonal being. Πρόσωπον indeed is the mask or the rôle of an actor: "the other" here is all on the surface, and as such it has no ontological density. Thus it is not surprising that the Fathers should have preferred to this weak and perhaps misleading word, a word without encumbrances, a word whose meaning they completely remodelled, that of ὑπόστασις.

While οὐσία seems to have been a philosophic word on its way to becoming vulgarized, ὑπόστασις was a popular word which was beginning to assume a philosophic sense. In everyday language, it designated subsistence, but among certain Stoics, it had assumed the sense of a distinct substance, of the individual. In the final analysis, οὐσία and ὑπόστασις were almost synonyms, both relating to being, the first denoting especially essence, the second, singularity, without, however, being able to press this divergence too far. (With Aristotle, indeed, the "first ousias" designated individual subsistences, and hypostasis, as St. John of Damascus was later to note, sometimes signified simply "existence.") This relative equivalence favored the elaboration of a Christian language. No pre-existing context would come to disrupt the equilibrium of the two terms whose equal dignity the Fathers wished to stress; they avoided the risk of giving the preponderance to impersonal essence. Ousia and hypostasis were, at the outset, practically synonyms, both being concerned with the sphere of being. The Fathers, by specializing their meaning, came to be able, without external hindrance, to root personhood in being, and to personalize ontology.

Ousia, in the Trinity, is not an abstract idea of divinity, a rational essence binding three divine individuals, as humanity for example is common to three men. Apophaticism gives it the metalogical depth of an unknowable transcendence; the Bible envelopes it in the glorious radiance of the divine names. As for hypostasis—and it is here, under the influence of Christianity, that a true advancement of thought emerges—it no longer contains anything individual. The individual is part of a species, or rather he is only a part of it: he divides the nature to which he belongs, he is the result of its atomization, so to say. There is nothing of the sort in the Trinity, where every hypostasis assumes in its fullness divine nature. Individuals are at once opposite and repetitive: each possesses its fraction of nature; but indefinitely divided, it is always the same nature, without authentic diversity. The hypostases, on the other hand, are infinitely united and infinitely different: they *are* the divine nature, but none possesses it, none breaks it to own it exclusively. It is precisely because each one opens itself to the others, because they share nature without restriction, that the latter is not divided. And this indivisible nature gives every hypostasis its depth, confirms its uniqueness, reveals itself in this unity of the unique, in this communion in which every person, without confusion, shares integrally in all the others: the more they are one the more they are diverse, since nothing of the communal nature escapes them; and the more they are diverse the more they are one, since their unity is not impersonal uniformity, but a fertile tension of irreducible diversity, an abundance of a "circumincession without mixture or confusion" (St. John of Damascus).

Trinitarian theology thus opens to us a new aspect of the human reality: that of personhood. Ancient philosophy was indeed ignorant of the meaning of personhood. Greek thought did not go beyond an "atomic" conception of the individual. Roman thought, going from the mask to the rôle, defined *persona* through juridical relationships. Only the revelation of the Trinity, unique foundation of Christian anthropology, could situate personhood in an absolute manner. For the Fathers, indeed, personhood is freedom in relation to nature: it eludes all conditioning, be it psychological or moral. Every attribute is repetitive, it belongs to nature and is found again among other individuals. Even a cluster of qualities can be found elsewhere. Personal uniqueness is what remains when one takes away all cosmic context, social and individual—all, indeed, that may be conceptualized. Eluding concepts, personhood cannot be defined. It is the incomparable, the wholly-other. One can only add up individuals, not persons. The person is always unique. The concept objectifies and collects. Only a thought methodically "deconceptualized" by apophasis can evoke the mystery of personhood. For that which remains irreducible to every nature cannot be defined, but only designated. It is only to be seized through a personal relationship, in a reciprocity analogous to that of the hypostases of the Trinity, in an unfolding which goes beyond the opaque banality of the world of individuals. For the approach to personhood is penetration into a personal universe, at once assumed and open-ended: that of the highest artistic creations, that above all, sometimes very humble but always unique, of a life offered and mastered.

The divine attributes relate to common nature: intelligence, will, love, peace concern the three hypostases together and cannot differentiate them. One cannot in an absolute way qualify each hypostasis with a divine name. We have said that personal uniqueness eludes every definition, that personhood can only be evoked in its relation with another. The only way to distinguish the hypostases will therefore be by making precise their relationships, and above all their relationship to the common source of divinity, to the "divinity-source" of the Father. "Not to be procreated, to be procreated, to proceed, characterize the Father, the Son and He Whom we call the Holy Spirit," writes Gregory of Nazianzus. The *innascibility* of the Father without beginning (this is the basic idea of the monarchy of the Father, the full importance of which we will soon see), the *generation* of the Son and the *procession* of the Holy Spirit—these are the relationships which allow us to distinguish the persons. But two remarks impose themselves here: the first is that these relationships indicate, but do not underlie the hypostatic diversity. Diversity is an absolute reality. It is rooted in the triple and primordial mystery of the divine persons, and our thought, which it precedes infinitely, cannot evoke it except in a negative way by declaring that the Father without beginning is neither the Son nor the Holy Spirit, that the procreated Son is neither the Holy Spirit nor the Father, that the Spirit proceeding from the Father is neither the Father nor the Son. The second remark is as follows: these relations are not relations of opposition as Latin theology affirms, but simple relations of diversity. They do not differentiate nature in persons, they confirm the absolute identity and the no less absolute diversity of the hypostases; and above all, in connection with each hypostasis, they are *ternary*, and can never result in the duality which is precisely implied by opposition. It is impossible indeed to fit one hypostasis into a dyad, impossible to evoke it without immediately causing the other two to rise up: the Father is such only in relation to the Son and the Spirit. As for the generation of the Son and the procession of the Spirit, they are in a certain way simultaneous, the one implying the other.

This denial of opposition and hence of duality is, regarding the Trinity, rather more the denial or, better, the surmounting of number. God is "identically monad and triad," said St. Maximus the Confessor. He is at once unitrinity and triunity, with the double equation of 1=3, of 3=1. In his treatise on the Holy Spirit, St. Basil evokes this "metamathematics": "In fact we do not count by adding, starting from unity to end with plurality, for we do not say: one and two and three, nor first, second and third. I am in fact the First God and I am the Last (Is. 44:6). And of a second God we have not yet heard tell until this day, for in adoring a God of Gods we confess the characteristic of hypostases and remain within the monarchy."

Surmounting of the monad: the Father *is* a total gift of His divinity to the Son and to the Spirit. Were He only monad, were He to identify with His essence instead of giving it, He would not fully be a person. That is why the God of the Old Testament is not the Father. Personal but closed upon Himself, He is all the more terrible for being able only to enter into a relationship with beings of another nature: whence His "tyrannical" appearance. Between Him and man there is no reciprocity. That is why St. Cyril of Alexandria considered that the name of Father is superior to that of God: for if God is such only for those who are not God, the Father is the Father in relation to the Son, Who is in no way inferior to Him. In the unfolding of the biblical monad, the name of Father reveals itself as an *interior* name of God.

The monad being unfolded, the personal plenitude of God

cannot stabilize itself upon a dyad, because two implies opposition and reciprocal limitation. Two would divide the divine nature and would locate within the infinite the root of the indefinite, the first polarity of a creation which would become, as in the gnostic systems, manifestation. Divine reality is therefore unthinkable in two persons. The surmounting of two, that is, of number, occurs in three: not a return to the origin but a blossoming of personal being. Three in fact is not here the sum of an addition. Three absolutely diverse realities cannot be counted; three Absolutes do not add up together. Three, beyond all calculation, beyond all opposition, establishes absolute diversity. Transcending number, it does not initiate nor enclose a series, but opens, beyond two, infinity: not the opacity of the in-itself, the absorption of a return to the One, but the open-ended infinity of the living God, the inexhaustible profusion of divine life. "The monad is set in motion by virtue of its richness; the dyad is surpassed, for divinity is above matter and form; the triad is enclosed within perfection, for it is the first to go beyond the composition of the dyad." The mystery that Gregory of Nazianzus evokes in these Plotinian terms opens to us another domain beyond all logic and all metaphysic. Faith here feeds and elevates thought beyond its limits unto a contemplation whose aim precisely is but to share in the divine life of the Trinity.

V. The Procession of Persons and the Divine Attributes

Christian theology does not know an abstract divinity: God cannot be conceived outside of the three persons. If "ousia" and "hypostasis" are almost synonyms it is in order to break our reason, to prevent us from objectifying divine essence outside of the persons and their "eternal movement of love" (St. Maximus the Confessor). The God of Christian theology is a concrete God, since unique divinity is at once common to the three hypostases and proper to each of them: to the Father as source, to the Son as procreated, to the Spirit as proceeding from the Father.

The term of "monarch" for the Father is current in the great theologians of the fourth century. It means that the very source of divinity is personal. The Father is divinity, but precisely because He is the Father, He confers it in its fullness on the two other persons. The latter take their origin from the Father, μόνη ἀρχή, single principle, whence the term "monarchy," the "divinity-source," as Dionysius the Areopagite says of the Father. It is from this indeed that springs—in this that is rooted—the identical, unshared, but differently communicated divinity of the Son and the Holy Spirit. The notion of monarchy therefore denotes in a single word the unity and the difference in God, *starting from a personal principle.* The greatest theologian of the Trinity, St. Gregory of Nazianzus, could only evoke this mystery through veritable poetry, alone capable of lifting one beyond words. "They are not divided in will," he writes, "they are not separated in power" nor in any other attribute. "In brief, divinity is not shared out among the sharers." "In three suns which penetrate one another, single would be the light," for the Word and the Spirit are two rays of the same sun, or "rather two new suns."

Thus the Trinity is the initial mystery, the Holy of Holies of the divine reality, the very life of the hidden God, of the living God. Only poetry can evoke it, precisely because it celebrates and does not pretend to explain. All existence and all knowledge are posterior to the Trinity and find in It their base. The Trinity cannot be grasped by man. It is rather the Trinity that seizes man and provokes praise in him. Outside of praise and adoration, outside of the personal relationship of faith, our language, when speaking of the Trinity, is always false. If Gregory the Theologian writes of the three that "They are not divided in will," it is because we cannot say that the Son has been procreated by the will of the Father. We cannot think the Father without the Son: He is Father-with-a-Son; it is thus from all eternity. There is no act in the Trinity, and to even speak of state would imply a passivity which would not be appropriate. "When we aspire to divinity, the first cause, the monarchy, the number *one* appears to us; and when we aspire after those in whom divinity lies and who proceed from the first principle in the same eternity and glory, we then adore the *three*" (St. Gregory of Nazianzus).

Does not the monarchy of the Father imply a certain subordination of the Son and the Spirit? No, for a principle can be perfect only if it is the principle of a reality equal to it. The Greek Fathers readily spoke of the "Father-cause," but this is merely an analogical term whose deficiency the purifying use of apophaticism enables us to measure. In our experience, the cause is superior to the effect. In God, on the contrary, the cause as fulfillment of personal love cannot produce inferior effects: it wishes them to be equal in dignity, and is therefore also the cause of their equality. Besides, in God there is no extraposition of cause and effect, but *causality within one and the same nature*. Causality here does not provoke an external effect as in the material world, nor an effect which is reabsorbed into its cause, as in the ontological hierarchies of India and Neo-Platonism; it is only the important image of an inexpressible communion. The Father "would only be the Principle (ἀρχὴ) of petty and ignoble things, but more than this, He would be the Principle only in a petty and undignified way, if He were not the Principle of divinity and goodness which one adores in the Son and the Holy Spirit: in the one as Son and Word, in the other as Spirit proceeding without separation" (St. Gregory of Nazianzus). The Father would not be a true person if He were not this: πρός, towards, entirely turned towards other persons, entirely communicated to those whom He makes persons, therefore equals, by the wholeness of His love.

The Trinity is therefore not the result of a process, but a primordial given. It has Its principle only in this, not above it: nothing is superior to It. Ἀρχή, the monarchy manifests itself only in, by and for the Trinity, in the relationship of the three, in a relation always ternary, to the exclusion of all opposition, of every dyad.

St. Athanasius had already affirmed that the generation of the Son is a work of nature. And St. John of Damascus, in the eighth century, was to distinguish the *work of nature*, which is generation and procession, and the *work of will*, which is the creation of the world. The work of nature, moreover, is not a work in the proper sense, but the very being of God, for God *is*, by His nature, Father, Son and Holy Spirit. God has no need to reveal Himself to Himself, by a sort of wakening of consciousness of the Father within the Son and the Spirit, as Bulgakov believed. Revelation is thinkable only in relation to the other-than-God, that is to say, within creation. Just as the trinitarian existence is not the result of an act of will, it is impossible to see here the process of an internal necessity.

One must therefore carefully distinguish the *causality* of the Father—which locates the three hypostases in their absolute diversity, though without the possibility of establishing any order between them—from its *revelation* or *manifestation*. The Spirit leads us, through the Son, to the Father, where we discover the unity of the three. The Father, according to the terminology of St. Basil, reveals Himself through the Son in the Spirit. Here is affirmed a process, an order from which issues that of the three names: Father, Son and Holy Spirit.

Likewise all the divine names, which communicate to us the life common to the three, come to us from the Father through the Son in the Holy Spirit. The Father is the source, the Son the manifestation, the Spirit the force which manifests. Thus the Father is the source of love, the Son, love which reveals itself, the Spirit, love realized in us. Or, according to the admirable formula of Metropolitan Philaret of Moscow, the Father is crucifying love, the Son, love crucified, the Spirit, love triumphant. The divine names are the flow of the divine life whose source is the Father, shown to us by the Son, and communicated to us by the Spirit.

Byzantine theology calls these divine names "energies." The word is particularly apt for this eternal radiance of the divine nature. Better than the "attributes" of scholarly theology, it evokes for us these living forces, these outbursts, these overflowings of the divine glory. For the theory of uncreated energies is profoundly biblical: the Bible often evokes the flaming and thunderous glory which makes God known outside of Himself, all the while hiding Him under a profusion of light. Cyril of Alexandria speaks of the splendour of the divine essence which is manifested. The luminous terms, which are not at all metaphorical here but express the experience of the highest contemplation, recur continually to denote the splendour of a dazzling beauty. The divine glory is multiform. "Jesus did many other things; if one were to write them down one by one, the whole world, I believe, could not contain the books one would write about them" (John 21:25).

Likewise the whole world could not contain the countless names of glory. "Δυνάμεις, Powers," said Pseudo-Dionysius: and sometimes he speaks in the singular, sometimes in the plural. The number here is of no consequence: not one, not several, but an infinity of divine names. God is wisdom, love, justice . . . not because He wishes it so, but because He is such. There is no masquerade here: God shows what He is. We cannot know the divine essence down to its deepest depths, but we know this radiance of glory which is truly God: for whether we call the divine nature "essence," in so far as it is inexhaustible transcendence, or "energy," in so far as it gloriously manifests itself, it is always the same nature. "Father, glorify me with this glory which I had before the world began" (John 17:5). The energetic manifestation does not therefore depend on creation: it is perpetual radiance, which is in no way conditioned by the existence or non-existence of the world. Certainly we discover it in the creature, for "since the creation of the world, the works [of God] render visible to intelligence His invisible attributes" (Romans 1:20): the creature is stamped with the seal of divinity. But this divine presence is a permanent glory, eternal, a non-contingent manifestation of essence, and as such unknowable. This is the light which from all eternity bathes the plenitude, perfect in itself, of trinitarian life.

Chapter Two

THE CREATION

I. Introduction

The world was created by the will of God. It is of another nature than God. It exists outside of God, "not by place but by nature" (St. John of Damascus). These simple affirmations of faith open onto a mystery as unfathomable as that of the divine being: the mystery of the created being, the reality of a being external to any presence of God, free in relation to His omnipotence, having an interiority radically new in face of the trinitarian plenitude, in brief the reality of the *other-than-God*, the irreducible ontological density of the *other*.

Christianity alone, or more precisely, the Judaeo-Christian tradition, knows the notion of absolute creation. Creation *ex nihilo* is a dogma of the faith. It finds its first expression in the Bible, in the second book of Maccabees (7:28) where a mother, exhorting her son to martyrdom, says to him: "Behold the heavens and the earth, and seeing all that is there, you will understand that God has created it from nothing" (ἐκ οὐκ ὄντων, according to the translation of the Septuagint). If one remembers that οὐκ is a radical negation which, by contrast with the other adverb of negation, μη, leaves no room for doubt, and that it is here used systematically against the rules of grammar, one can measure the total implication of the expression: God has not created starting from something, but starting with what is not, from "nothingness."

There is nothing remotely similar in other religions or metaphysics. Sometimes creation is said to begin with a possibility of being permanently open to demiurgic ordering:

such was the prime matter of ancient thought, which immutable being was said to inform. This matter does not exist in itself. It is a pure possibility of being, non-being certainly, but the μη ὄν, which is not the absolute nothingness, οὐκ ὄν. By reflection, it receives a certain verisimilitude, a precarious evocation of the world of ideas. Of such in particular is Platonic dualism, but also, with certain differences, the perpetual taking-of-form of matter in Aristotle.

Sometimes we encounter the idea of creation as a divine procession. God brings forth from His own being, often by a primordial polarization which gives rise to the multiform universe. On this understanding the world is manifestation or emanation of divinity. Such is the fundamental conception of India, which we find again in the Hellenic world with gnosticism and to which the thought of Plotinus, which tends towards a monism, is very close. Here cosmogony becomes a theogony: the absolute becomes relative through stages of descending "condensation," it manifests and downgrades itself in the universe. The world is a fallen God who strains to become God again. Its origin resides sometimes in a mysterious catastrophe which one may call the fall of God, sometimes in an inner necessity, in a strange cosmic passion where God seeks to assume consciousness of Himself, sometimes in a cyclic temporality of manifestations and reabsorptions which seem to be imposed upon God Himself.

In neither of the two cases does the idea of a creation *ex nihilo* exist. For in Christianity, matter itself is created. This mysterious matter which Plato said only bastard concepts could grasp, this pure possibility of being, is itself created, as St. Augustine has remarkably well demonstrated. And on the other hand, how could creation have an uncreated substratum, how could it be God doubled, since it is by essence the *other-than-God*?

Creation is therefore a free act, a gratuitous act of God. It does not respond to any necessity of divine being whatever. Even moral motivations which are sometimes attributed to it are platitudes without importance: the God-Trinity is plenitude of love; It has no need of another to pour out Its love, since the other is already in It, in the circumincession of the hypostases. God is therefore creator because He wishes it thus: the name of creator is secondary in relation to the three names of the Trinity. God is eternally Trinity. He is not eternally creator, as Origen believed, who, prisoner of the cyclic conceptions of antiquity, therefore made Him dependent on the creature. If the idea of creation as a totally free act embarrasses us, it is because our thought, being vitiated by sin, identifies liberty and license. God therefore seems to us a whimsical tyrant. But if for us liberty, when it does not adhere to the laws of creation within which we find ourselves, is an evil license which disintegrates being, for God, who transcends creation, liberty is infinitely good: it gives rise to being. In creation, indeed, we recognize order, finality, love—all the very opposite of license. The qualities of God, which have nothing to do with our dissolute pseudo-liberty, here manifest themselves. The very being of God is reflected in the creature and calls it to share in His divinity. This call and the possibility of responding to it constitute for those who are within creation the only justification of the latter.

The creation *ex nihilo* is the work of the will of God. That is why St. John of Damascus opposes it to the generation of the Word: "Since the generation," he says, "is a work of nature and proceeds from the very substance of God, it must needs be without beginning and eternal, for otherwise the begetting would be subject to change and there would be a God before and another God after; God would suffer increase. As for creation, it is the work of the will of God, therefore it is not coeternal with God. For it cannot be that what is brought forth from nothingness could be coeternal with that which exists without origin and always." This work is contingent: God might not have created. But, contingent in relation to the very being of the Trinity, it imposes on created beings the necessity to exist, and to exist for ever: contingent for God, creation is necessary for itself, because God freely makes of the created being what it must be.

Thus the positive meaning of divine gratuitousness appears to us. This is, to speak by analogy (but this analogy constitutes the very meaning of creation), the gratuitousness of the poet. "Poet of the heavens and of the earth," one could call God, translating word for word the Greek text of the Credo. Thus can we penetrate the mystery of the created being. To create is not to reflect oneself in a mirror, even that of prime matter, it is not vainly to divide oneself in order to take everything unto oneself. It is a calling forth of *newness*. One might almost say: a risk of newness. When God raises, outside of Himself, a new subject, a free subject, that is the peak of His creative act. Divine freedom is accomplished through creating this supreme risk: another freedom.

That is why one cannot objectify the original nothing. "*Nihil*," means here simply that "before" creation nothing existed "outside" of God. Or rather that this "outside" and this "before" are absurd, since it is precisely the creation which posits them. To think this "outside" is to knock against nothing, that is to say, no longer to be able to think. It exists only through the creation, it is this "spacing-out" ("*espacement*") itself which constitutes the creation. Similarly, one cannot evoke what existed "before" the creation: the "beginning" has no meaning in God; it is born with the created being, it is creation which constitutes time, of which "before" and "after" are expressions. Like "outside," "before" returns to "*nihil*" and stifles thought. The one and the other, the Germans would say, are "limit concepts." Thus the whole dialectic of being and nothingness is absurd: nothingness has no existence of its own (it would anyway be a contradiction *in adjecto*); it is correlative to the very being of creatures; the latter are founded neither in themselves nor in the divine essence, but uniquely on the will of God. Stability, permanency for the creature is therefore its relation to God. In relation to itself it amounts to nothing.

The "newness" of creation adds nothing, therefore, to the being of God. Our concepts proceed by juxtaposition, according to a "thingist" imagery, but one cannot add up God and the world. Thought must proceed here by analogy, in a manner designed to emphasize at once the relation and the difference; for the creature exists only in God, in this creative will which precisely makes it different from God, that is to say, makes it "creature." "Creatures are poised on the creative word of God as on a diamond bridge; beneath the abyss of divine infinity, above the abyss of their own nothingness" (Philaret of Moscow).

II. The Creative Trinity and Divine Ideas

Creation is the work of the Trinity. The Credo names the Father "creator of heaven and earth," the Son "He through whom all things were made," the Holy Spirit "creator of life," ζωοποιόν. The will is common to the three, and it is this that creates: the Father can therefore not be creator unless the Son and the Spirit are also creators. The Father creates through the Word in the Holy Spirit, says the patristic adage, and St. Irenaeus calls the Son and the Spirit "the two hands of God." This is the economic manifestation of the Trinity. The three Persons create together, but each one in a way which is His own, and the created being is the fruit of their collaboration. According to St. Basil, the Father is "the primordial cause of everything that has been made," the Son "the operative cause," the Spirit "the perfecting cause." Rooted in the Father, the action of the Trinity is presented as the double economy of the Son and of the Spirit: the former making the desire of God come into existence, the latter accomplishing it in goodness and beauty; the one calling the creature to lead it to the Father (and His call confers on it its ontological density), the other helping the creature to respond to this call and communicating perfection to it.

When the Fathers treat of the economical manifestation of the Trinity, rather than the name of Son, which denotes intra-trinitarian relationships, they prefer that of Word. The Word indeed is revelation, the manifestation of the Father: of someone, in consequence, who binds the notion of the Word to the domain of economy. St. Gregory of Nazianzus analyses in his Fourth Theological Oration this function of the Word. The Son is the Logos, he says, because, while remaining united to the Father, He reveals Him. The Son defines the Father. "The Son is therefore a brief and simple declaration of the nature of the Father."

Every created thing has its "logos," its "essential reason": and, says St. Gregory, "can anything exist which does not lean on the divine Logos?" Nothing exists which is not founded on the Logos, the *raison d'être par excellence*. By It has everything been made; It gives to the created world not only the order signified by Its name, but its very ontological reality. The Logos is the divine hearth whence fly the creative rays, the "logoi" peculiar to creatures, these causative words of God which at once raise up and name all beings. Every being therefore has its "idea," its "reason" in God, in the thought of the Creator who produces not through caprice, but with "reason" (and this is yet another meaning of Logos). Divine ideas are the eternal reasons of creatures. Here the thought of the Fathers seems to take on a Platonic resonance. Are we in the presence of a Christian Platonism? A brief comparison will allow us to understand that the Fathers, if they have used certain elements of Greek philosophy, have entirely renewed their content, in the final account much more biblical than Platonic.

In Plato, the "ideas" represent the very sphere of Being. The sensible world has no verity, only a verisimilitude: it is only real so far as it participates in the ideas. To contemplate the latter, one must escape the precarious universe of change, the flux of generation and corruption. Ideas represent therefore the superior level of being, not God but the Divine. The "daemons," the gods, are indeed inferior to them. The "creation" of which the *Timaeus* speaks remains a myth, for the world has always existed: eternally the "demiurge" shapes it by copying it from the model of the ideal world, the true world. Neo-Platonism, which according to the expression of Jean Wahl, "hypostasizes the hypotheses of Plato," establishes the ineffable One above the κόσμος νοητός: the ideas, henceforth, are those of divine Intelligence, of this νοῦς which emanates from the absolute superior to being itself. St. Augustine, after having read extracts from the *Enneads* translated into Latin, allowed himself to be fascinated by these themes of Plotinus. But the Greek Fathers, who knew the philosophers much better, mastered their thought far more easily, and used it in all freedom. For them, God is not only an intelligence containing divine ideas: His essence infinitely transcends ideas. It is a free and personal God who creates all by His will and His wisdom; and the ideas of all things are contained in this will and this wisdom, and not in the divine essence. The Greek Fathers have consequently refused both to introduce the intelligible world into the interior being of God and to separate this, the intelligible world, from the sensible. Their feeling for the divine being has made them reject an intelligible God, while their feeling for the created being has forbidden them to reduce Him to a bad copy. St. Augustine himself, at the end of his life in his *Retractions*, rejected the dualism implicit in his static "exemplarism": there are not two worlds, he then affirmed. However, his teaching about the ideas contained in the very being of God, at once as determination of essence and as exemplary causes of creatures, impressed itself upon Western theology and holds a major place in Thomistic systematics. For Orthodoxy, on the contrary, it is unthinkable that God, in order to create, should be content to produce a replica of His own thought, finally of Himself. It would be to withdraw from the created world its originality and value, depreciate creation and hence God as creator. And the whole Bible, and particularly the Book of Job, the Psalms, the Proverbs, emphasize the absolute and splendid newness of creation, before which angels utter cries of joy—the Creation-Benediction of Genesis, Creation-Play of Wisdom, "hymn most marvelously composed to the all-powerful force," as St. Gregory of Nyssa writes.

The Greek Fathers therefore have seen in Platonism the discovery, partial and dangerous, of a reality: not dualism, but the transparency of the visible to the invisible. They have not hesitated to use its language, to speak of "paradigms" and "ideas." But they have impregnated this language with a thoroughly biblical respect for the sensible and the living God. They bring the Logos closer to the "word" which the Psalms evoke, and above all to those creative words resounding in Genesis. The ideas then are no longer a necessary determination of divine being, but the creative will, the living word of God. They no longer constitute a "hinterworld," but the very depth of the creature, its method of participating in divine energy, its vocation to the highest love. The creative will of God implies order and reason; it inseminates with living ideas the "spacing-out" of the creation; it demands for its diffusion an "outside" of the divine nature. St. John of Damascus in his account of "the orthodox faith" speaks thus of creation in terms of ideas-wills, or rather of volitional thoughts. Thus the divine ideas are inseparable from the creative intention. Without doubt God has eternally thought the world, but only in relation to this "other" which must "begin," that is to say, lay the foundations of time. Thus according to the Scriptures, it is Wisdom which positions the seven pillars of the mansion. The ideal world of Plato is here turned about: it is an instrument of creation, not a world beyond it. God in order to create, thinks creation, and this thought gives its reality to the being of things. The ideas are Wisdom in the divine work, or rather, are Wisdom at work: exemplarism if one so wishes, but dynamic, that of a will-thought, or a will-word in which are rooted the "logoi" of things. By the divine Word the world is suspended over its own nothingness, and there is one word for each thing, one word in each thing, which represents its norm of existence and its way to transfiguration. The saint whose created will cooperates freely with the will-idea of God Who at once establishes and solicits it, perceives, through the detached contemplation of nature, the world as "a musical arrangement": in each thing he hears a word of the Word, the thing being no more for him, in this fervent deciphering of "the book of the world," than an existing word, for "heaven and earth may pass away, but my words will not pass away" (Matt. 24:35).

III. Creation: Time and Eternity

"In the beginning was the Word," writes St. John, and

Genesis affirms: "In the beginning God created the heaven and the earth." Origen identifies these two documents: "God," he says, "created everything in His Word, thus through all eternity in Himself." Meister Eckhart makes the same identification: the principle evoked in the double *in principio* is for him God as intellect containing the Word as well as the world. Arius, on the contrary, confusing the Greek homonyms γέννησις, birth, and γένεσις, creation, interprets St. John in terms of Genesis, and transforms the Son into a creature.

The Fathers, to underline both the unknowability of the divine essence and the divinity of the Son, have distinguished between these two beginnings: a distinction between the work of nature, primordial being of God, and the work of will, implying relation with the other which is set up by this relation itself. St. John thus evokes an eternal "beginning," that of the Word: the term here is analogical and denotes an eternal relationship. On the other hand, "beginning" assumes its full sense in the Genesis text, where the calling forth of the world gives rise to time. Ontologically, Genesis is thus second compared to St. John's Prologue: the "two beginnings" are different without being for all that completely foreign to each other, if we remember the intentional nature of the divine ideas, of the Wisdom, at once eternal and yet turned towards this "other" which, properly speaking, must have a beginning. For Wisdom itself proclaims: "The Lord has had me as first fruit of His ways, as prelude of His works, since all time" (Prov. 8:22). The "beginning" of the first verse of Genesis thus signifies the creation of time. In this way, the relation of time and eternity is established, a problem which joins that of creation *ex nihilo*.

One must here dispose of two obstacles. The first would be that of being "Greek," that is, being pure metaphysician when confronted with biblical data and trying to reduce through reason the mystery of their symbolism, to the point of rendering useless the "leap of faith." Theology does not have to beg explanations from philosophers: it alone can answer their problems, not against mystery and faith, but by nurturing the intellection of the mystery, by transforming it, through faith, in a total commitment of the person. True theology goes beyond and transfigures metaphysics.

But the other obstacle would be, through hatred for philosophers, to be solely "Jew," that is, to take literally the concrete symbolism of the Scripture. Certain modern exegetes, mostly (but not only) Protestants, want very carefully to banish from their thought everything, however little, that smacks of philosophy. Thus, Oscar Cullmann in his book *Christ and Time* aspires to reject as Platonic or Hellenic all problems of eternity and to bring the Bible down to its bare text. Now the Bible has depth: but its most ancient parts, particularly Genesis, proceed according to an archaic logic which does not separate the concrete from the abstract, the image from the idea, the symbol from the symbolized reality. Poetic logic, if you wish, or sacramental, one whose simplicity is only apparent, pregnant as it is with a Word that gives to the flesh (inseparably from words and things) an incomparable transparency. Our language is no longer such: less total perhaps, but more conscious and more rigorous, it divests archaic intellection of its fleshly envelope. It grasps it at the level of thought: not of ratiocination, one must repeat, but of contemplative intellection. A modern man, if he interprets the Bible, must thus have the courage to think: for one does not act like a child with impunity. If one refuses to abstract at depth, one nonetheless abstracts, by the very virtue of using language; but one abstracts at the surface, and thus one ends, not with the childlike wonderment of the archaic writer, but with infantile positions. Then eternity becomes linear, like time; one thinks of it as an indefinite line! And the temporal existence of the world, from creation to the parousia, is but a finite portion of this line. Eternity thus reduces to a time without beginning or end, the infinite reduces to the indefinite. But what becomes then of transcendence? To underline the poverty of this philosophy (for such it finally is) it suffices to remember that the finite is not commensurable with the infinite.

Neither Greek nor Jew, but Christian, the Fathers gave to this problem an answer that, far from blaspheming the Bible through ratiocination or platitude, seizes it in its depth.

For St. Basil, the first moment of time is not yet time. "As the beginning of a road is not yet the road, nor the beginning of a house, a house, thus the beginning of time is not yet time, nor even a minimal part of time." This first moment, for us, is unthinkable—if, that is, we weakly define the instant as a point in time (a false representation, as St. Augustine has shown, since the future becomes past without ceasing, without our ever being able to grasp the present in time). Now the first moment is not divisible. It is not even infinitely small, but without measure according to time: it is the moment as limit, thus without duration.

What then is the moment? This problem preoccupied ancient thought. In the impasse of a ruthless rationality, Zeno reduced time to the absurd, since it was—or rather could not be—at once movement and rest. More aware of mystery, Plato had remarkable thoughts on the "instant" which, he said, is not time but a limit, and, as such, an opening onto eternity. The present without dimension, without duration, revealed itself as the presence of eternity.

For St. Basil this is precisely that first moment in which the entire assemblage of being appeared, symbolized by "the heavens and the earth." The creature rises up in an "instant" which is at once eternal and temporal, on the frontier of eternity and time. The "beginning," logically analogous to the geometric notion of the frontier (between two planes, for example) is a sort of instantaneousness, non-temporal in itself, but whose creative explosion gives rise to time. This is the point of contact of the divine will with what will henceforth become and endure: the very origin of the creature is thus a change, a "beginning" and that is why time is a form of created being, whereas eternity properly belongs to God. But this original contingency in no way belittles the created being: the creature will never disappear, for the word of God is unshakeable (I Peter 1:25). The world thus created will always exist, even when time is abolished, or rather, since time itself is a creature, when it is transformed into the eternal newness of the apocatastasis.

Thus are joined in the same mystery the first and the eighth day, which coincide in Sunday. For the latter is both the first and the eighth day of the week, that of the entrance to eternity. The weekly cycle closes on Saturday in the divine rest of the Sabbath. Beyond that, Sunday, the day of the creation and recreation of the world, the day of the Resurrection, is like the "instant" of eternity, that of the first and last limit. More even than the Alexandrians, Basil has developed these notions, stressing that, in the presence of this mystery, one must not kneel on Sunday, since on that day one escapes the slave's temporalness to enter symbolically into the Kingdom where the upright man, the saved man, participates in the brotherhood of the Resurrected.

One must thus avoid the categories of time when one evokes eternity. If however, the Bible uses them, it is to underline by means of a rich symbolism the positiveness of time, where ripen the encounters of God and man, its ontological autonomy as an adventure of human freedom, its possibility of transfiguration. The Fathers have well sensed this, and have guarded themselves against defining eternity *a contrario* from time. If the categories of time are movement, change, transition from one state to another, one cannot contrast them term for term with immobility, unchangeability, the invariability of a static eternity: that would be the eternity of Plato's intelligible world, not that of the living God. If God lives in eternity, this living eternity must go beyond the opposition of mobile time and immobile eternity. St. Maximus stresses that the eternity of the intelligible world is *a created eternity*: portions, truths, the unchanging structures of the cosmos, the geometry of ideas which govern creation, network of mathematical essences, this is the *aeon*, aeonic eternity, which began like time (whence its name: for it takes its beginning "in the age," ἐν αἰῶνι, in passing from non-being to being), but which remains unchanging, subject to an intemporal existence. This aeonic eternity is stable; it is what makes the world coherent and intelligible. Sensible and intelligible, time and aeon cling together, for, both having a beginning, they are commensurables. The aeon is immobile time, time is the moving aeon. And only their coexistence, their interpenetration, can make time thinkable.

The aeon bears a close relation to the angelic world.

Angels and men both participate in time and in the aeon, but in a different fashion. While the human condition is temporal, but in a time made intelligible by the aeon, the angels have known the free choice of time only at the moment of their creation: a sort of instantaneous temporality whence they emerge for an aeon of praise and service, or of revolt and hate. A process, however, exists in the aeon, since the angelic nature can grow ceaselessly with the acquisition of eternal benefits, but without temporal succession. Thus the angels present themselves as intelligible universes who participate in the organizing function of aeonic eternity.

As for divine eternity, that can be defined neither as the change belonging to time nor as the immutability belonging to the aeon. It transcends them both. The recourse necessary to apophasis forbids us to think of the living God according to the eternity of mathematical laws.

Thus Orthodox theology does not know of any uncreated intelligible. Otherwise, corporeality, alone created, would appear as a relative evil. The uncreated surpasses all oppositions, notably those of the intelligible and the sensible, of the temporal and the eternal. And the problem of time brings us back to this nothingness from which the divine will raises us to introduce an other-than-God into eternity.

IV. Creation: Cosmic Order

"In the beginning, God created heaven and earth." The heaven and earth in question on the first day of creation are not those that we see: for the one only appears with the "firmament" on the second day, or even with the "luminaries" on the fourth, and the other only with the separation of the dry land on the third. "Heaven and earth" of the first day signify the entirety of the universe, the visible and the invisible, the intelligible and the corporeal. Heaven: that is, the whole immensity of the spiritual worlds that surround our terrestrial being, the innumerable angelic spheres. The narrative of Genesis mentions them, then appears to lose interest in them, to speak only of the earth. Some brief indications about these spiritual universes are marked out, but not lingered over, in the two Testaments. Thus St. Gregory of Nyssa saw a symbol of angelic pleroma in the ninety-nine sheep left in the hills; the hundredth, the lost sheep, would be our terrestrial world. Indeed, in our fallenness, we cannot even place our world amidst these spiritual immensities.

This relative silence of the Scriptures is significant. It underlines the central importance of the earth, it defines a geocentrism. This is not the residue of a primitive cosmology (to what extent anyway are such cosmologies not symbolic?) which would keep faith with our post-Copernican universe. For this is not a physical geocentrism, but a spiritual one: the earth is *spiritually central* because it is the body of man, and because man, penetrating the indefiniteness of the visible to bind it again to the invisible, is the central being of creation, the being who reunites in himself the sensible and the intelligible and thus participates, richer than the angels, in all the orders of "earth" and of "heaven." At the center of the universe beats the heart of man, and only the saint whose purified heart encircles the most distant nebulae can know if these "starry spheres" are not like the reflection of angelic aeons, and, in consequence, have no need of salvation.

The mysteries of the divine economy are thus unfurled on earth, and that is why the Bible wants to bind us to the earth. Not only does it forbid us to lose ourselves in cosmic immensities (which our fallen nature cannot grasp anyway, except in their aspect of disintegration), not only does it want to win us from the usurpation of fallen angels and bind us to God alone, but when it speaks to us of angels, it shows them to us turned towards terrestrial history where divine economy inserts itself, as servants (or adversaries) of this economy.

Thus the six days of Genesis describe for us in a geocentric fashion the unfurling of creation. These six days, which are symbolized by those of the week, are stages less chronological than hierarchical. Differentiating elements simultaneously created on the first day, they define the concentric spheres of being at the center of which man, who virtually recapitulates them, finds himself.

"For the earth (here the whole of our cosmos) was deserted and void, darkness covered the abyss": it is the mixture of still undifferentiated elements. "The spirit of God hovered over the waters": like a brooding bird, says St. Basil, and the waters here indicate (as in baptism) the plasticity of the elements.

"God said: let there be light, and there was light." This was the first order given by God: the Word introduces Itself into the elementary, and gives rise to the first "information" of being, the light. Light is therefore the perfection of created being, the "luminous-force," raised by the "logoi-wills" which radiate from the Word and go to fertilize the darkness: less physical vibration in consequence than intellectual light.

And God gives rise to the polarity of light and darkness. "God scatters the light and the darkness." These belong to created being and one must not confuse them with the original "nothing," that mysterious limit to which one would then be giving a gross substantiality. The darkness ("God called the darkness 'night' "), which appears in the last phase of this "first day," is the potential moment of created being. It represents a wholly good reality, fruitful, like the earth which germinates the seed. God has not produced evil: there is no place in the first being for negative darkness. The positive darkness of the first day expresses the uterine mystery of fertility, the principle of the mystery of life proper to the earth and to the womb, to all that generates in the positive sense of the word, to every substance of life.

On the second day, God definitively separated the inferior water from the superior, that is to say the earthly cosmos, limited by the "firmament," from the angelic aeons of which Genesis henceforth will speak no more.

On the third day, by God's command, the cosmic elements whose indistinctiveness was symbolized by the waters, begin to separate. The waters in the proper sense collect together; the earth appears. It receives the order to produce plants, that is to say the first form of life. And the earth obeys the Logos, principle of life, at once the second person of the Trinity and the ordering power of the entire Trinity.

On the fourth day, appear the stars and their regular revolution: the order of the Logos is inscribed in the order of the visible sky. Life, awakened on the preceding "day," necessitates time, the rhythm of day and night. The creative simultaneousness of the first days becomes, for the creature, a succession.

On the fifth day, the Word creates fishes and birds: it is water, the moist element that receives the order to produce them. A curious kinship is thus established between the beings that swim and those that fly (whose shapes in fact do have some similarity), between water and air, both being fluid and moist. We sense very clearly here that it is not a question of a scientific cosmogony, in the modern sense of the term, but of another vision of being and of its hierarchies, a vision for which the mystery of form, the secondary qualities of the sensible (so greatly neglected by science) have a decisive meaning which hark back to the intelligible depths, the "logoi" of creation. This vision has become very difficult for our fallen nature, but we can find it again in the ecclesiastical "new creation," both in the liturgical and sacramental cosmos and in the liturgical θεωρία φυσικὴ of the ascetics.

On the sixth day, the element earth receives in its turn the order to produce animals. But suddenly the tone of the narrative changes; a new style of creation emerges. "Let us make," says God. What does this change signify? The creation of angelic spirits was done "in silence" (St. Isaac). The first word was light. Then God ordered and blessed ("God saw that it was good"). But on the sixth day, after the creation of the animals, when God said "Let us make man in Our image and according to Our likeness," it seemed that He stopped Himself and that the persons of the Trinity were in consort. The plural number that appears now shows that God is not alone. It is the deliberation of the "Divine Council" which proves that creation was the work neither of necessity nor of arbitrariness, but a free and reflective act. But why does the creation of man demand, instead of a simple order to the earth as with the animals, this council of the Three? This is because man, a personal being, needs the affirmation of the personal aspect of God in whose image he is made. The orders of God give rise to the different parts of created being. But man is not a part, since a person contains everything within himself. Free totality, he is born of the "reflection" of God as free totality.

"And God created man in His own image; He created him in the image of God; He created them male and female." Thus the mystery of the singular and plural in man reflects the mystery of the singular and plural in God: in the same way that the personal principle in God demands that the one nature express itself in the diversity of persons, likewise in man, created in the image of God. Human nature cannot be the possession of a monad. It demands not solitude but communion, the wholesome diversity of love. Then the divine order, "Be fruitful, multiply, fill the earth and subdue it," establishes a certain correspondence between sexuality and cosmic domination of the first couple and the mysterious overcoming in God of duality by the triad. But this paradisiacal "eros" would have been as different from our fallen and devouring sexuality as the sacerdotal royalty of man over created being should be from our actual devouring of each other. For God is precise: "And to all the wild beasts . . . I give all the green plants to eat." The narrative of creation, let us not forget, is expressed in the categories of the fallen world. But the Fall has changed the very meaning of the words. Sexuality, this "multiplying" that God orders and blesses, appears in our universe as irremediably linked to separation and death. This is because the condition of man has known, at least in his biological reality, a catastrophic mutation. But human love would not be pregnant with such a paradisiacal nostalgia if there did not remain painfully within it the memory of a first condition where the other and the world were known from the *inside*, where, accordingly, death did not exist.

"And God saw all that He had made, and behold, it was very good": a redoubled blessing *which, however, assimilates man to the other terrestrial creatures also appearing on the sixth day.*

Then, after the narrative of the creation which constitutes the first chapter of Genesis, a new narrative intervenes with the second chapter. The unfurling of creation is found there exposed in wholly different terms. For biblical criticism, it means a juxtaposition of diverse traditions, of two narratives in fact separated and sewn together afterwards. This is without doubt true at the material level of the formation of the text, but for us this very juxtaposition is the work of the Holy Spirit: there is no randomness in the Bible and everything is charged with meaning. The Bible is not born of human will, nor of human contingencies, but of the Holy Spirit which gives it its deep coherence. One cannot separate the Bible from Church, nor understand it outside of Her. What interests us is therefore not to know how two narratives of the creation found themselves thus joined, but why, and what deep meaning is concealed by their proximity.

And indeed, whereas the first narrative assimilates man to the other creatures of the earth in a common blessing, and at the level of nature stresses the anthropocosmic unity, the second narrative clearly defines the place of man. Its perspective is totally different in fact: man appears there not only as the summit, but also as the *principle* of creation. From the beginning, we learn that plants did not exist because man had still not been created: "There was no man to work the soil." Afterwards man's creation is reported to us in detail: "Then God made man from the dust of the earth and breathed life into him, and man became a living soul." Man is thus wrought by God Himself, by His hands, stressed the Fathers, and not raised up only by His Word (which brings us back to the "Council" in the first narrative, since the Son and the Holy Spirit, according to St. Irenaeus, are the "two hands" of God), and it is God's own breath that transforms this clay into a "living soul." Certain people have wished to see in this "living soul" the spiritual soul of man, and thus make of our intellect an emanation from God. But if our soul was uncreated, we would be God

Himself, burdened only by the earth's clay, and all creation would be but an illusory game. And yet St. Gregory of Nazianzus can speak, and rightly so, of the presence in man of a "particle of divinity." *This means that uncreated grace is implicated in the creative act itself, and that the soul receives at once life and grace: for grace is the breath of God, the "current of divinity," the vivifying presence of the Holy Spirit.* If man starts to live when God breathes life into him, it is because the grace of the Holy Spirit is the real principle of our existence. (As for the relation breath-nostrils, consequently human breath and respiration of God, it is based on the concrete symbolism of biblical cosmology, and does not represent a metaphor but a real analogy which still finds its application today in orthodox ascesis.)

The animal world, in this second narrative, appears after man and in relation to him, so that he should be no longer alone but should have "a helpmeet similar to himself." And Adam names the animals that God brings to him. For the world is made by God so as to be perfected by man. And man knows living beings from within; he specifies their secret; he orders their abundance; poet as he is priest, poet for God, since God "brought them to man *to see* what he would call them." Then, language coincided with the very being of things, and this paradisiacal language, irremediably lost, is not found again by the seeker of occultism, but only by those "charitable hearts" spoken of by Isaac the Syrian, those hearts "which are aflame with love for all of creation . . . for the birds, for the beasts, for all creatures." And the wild animals live in peace around the saints, as when Adam named them.

Man thus appears, in this second narrative of creation, to be the hypostasis of the terrestrial cosmos: terrestrial nature continues his body. But only a being of the very same nature as man's could be his helper, "a helpmeet similar to himself." Then God made man fall into an ecstatic slumber, and from the most intimate part of his nature (the symbolic "rib" close to his heart) made woman and brought her to man: and man recognized that Eve was "consubstantial" with him, "bone of his bones and flesh of his flesh." The Fathers relate the procession of the Holy Spirit with what they call the "procession" of Eve, different from Adam yet of the same nature as him: unity of nature and plurality of persons which evoke for us the mysteries of the New Testament. Just as the Spirit is not inferior to Him from Whom It proceeds, just so woman is not inferior to man: for love demands equality and love alone wished this primordial polarization, source of all the diversity of the human species.

V. Image and Likeness

Ancient philosophy understood the central condition of man and expressed it through the nature of the "microcosm." For the Stoics in particular, if man is superior to the cosmos, that is because he sums it up and gives it meaning: for the cosmos is a large man just as man is a small cosmos.

The idea of the microcosm has been taken up again by the Fathers, but with a vigorous bypassing of all immanentism. "There is nothing remarkable," said St. Gregory of Nyssa, "in man being the image and likeness of the universe: for the earth passes away, the sky changes, and all that is contained therein is as transient as that which contains it." Faced with the cosmic magics of declining antiquity, the simile affirms liberty: "In thinking to exalt human nature through this imposing name," Gregory adds, "they did not notice that man has found himself invested at the same time with the qualities of mosquitoes and mice." The true greatness of man is not in his incontestable kinship with the universe, but in his participation in divine plenitude, in the mystery within himself of the "image" and the "likeness." "In my quality of earth, I am attached to life here below," writes St. Gregory of Nazianzus, "but being also a divine particle, I bear in my breast the desire for a future life."

Man is a personal being like God, and not a blind nature. Such is the character of the divine image in him. His relationship with the universe finds itself somehow inverted when compared with the conceptions of antiquity: instead of becoming "disindividualized" to become "cosmic" and to merge thus in a divine impersonal, his absolute correspondence of person with a personal God allows him to "personalize" the world. Man no longer saves himself through the universe, but the universe is saved through man. For man is the hypostasis of the whole cosmos which participates in his nature. And the earth finds its personal meaning, hypostatic in man. To the universe, man is the hope of receiving grace and uniting with God, and also the danger of failure and fallenness. "Creation anxiously awaits this revelation of the sons of God," writes St. Paul. "It is indeed to vanity that creation was made subject, not willingly, but because of him who subjected it; with, however, the hope that creation would also be liberated from the slavery of corruption to participate in the glorious liberty of the children of God" (Rom. 8:19-21). Subjected to disorder and death by man, creation also attends upon man, become sons of God through grace, for its liberation.

The world follows man, since it is like him in nature: "the anthroposphere," one could say. And this anthropocosmic link is accomplished when that of the human image is accomplished, with God its prototype: for the person cannot, without destroying himself, aspire to possession of his nature, his quality notably of microcosm in the world, but discovers his fullness when he gives it, when he assumes the universe to offer it to God.

We are therefore responsible for the world. We are the word, the logos, through which it bespeaks itself, and it depends solely on us whether it blasphemes or prays. Only through us can the cosmos, like the body that it prolongs, receive grace. For not only the soul, but the body of man is created in the image of God. "Together they were created in the image of God," writes St. Gregory Palamas.

The image, then, cannot be objectified, "naturalized" we might say, by being attributed to some part or other of the human being. To be in the image of God, the Fathers affirm, in the last analysis is to be a personal being, that is to say, a free responsible being. Why, one may ask, did God create man free and responsible? Precisely because He wanted to call him to a supreme vocation: deification; that is to say, to become by grace, in a movement boundless as God, that which God is by His nature. And this call demands a free response; God wishes that this movement be a movement of love. Union without love would be automatic, and love implies freedom, the possibility of choice and refusal. Of course, there is a non-personal love, the blind movement of desire, slave of a natural force. But such is not the love of man or of angel for God: else we would be animals that attach themselves to God through a sort of obscure quasi-sexual attraction. To be what one must in loving God, one must admit that one can be the opposite; one must admit that one can revolt. The resistance of freedom alone gives sense to the union. The love that God claims is not physical magnetism, but the living tension of opposites. This freedom comes from God: it is the seal of our divine participation, the masterpiece of the Creator.

A personal being is capable of loving someone more than his own nature, more than his own life. The person, that is to say, the image of God in man, is then man's freedom with regard to his nature, "the fact of being freed from necessity and not being subject to the domination of nature, but able to determine oneself freely" (St. Gregory of Nyssa). Man acts most often under natural impulses. He is conditioned by his temperament, his character, his heredity, cosmic or psycho-social ambiance, indeed, his very historicity. But the truth of man is beyond all conditioning; and his dignity consists in being able to liberate himself from his nature, not by consuming it or abandoning it to itself, like the ancient or oriental sage, but by transfiguring it in God.

The goal of freedom, as St. Gregory of Nazianzus explains, is that the good belongs in truth to him who chooses it. God does not wish to remain in possession of the good He has created. He awaits from man more than a blind, entirely natural participation. He wants man consciously to assume his nature, to possess it freely as good, to recognize with gratitude in life and in the universe the gifts of divine love.

Personal beings constitute the peak of creation, since they can become God by free choice and grace. With them, the divine omnipotence raises up a radical "intervention," an integral newness: God creates beings who like Him can—let us recall the Divine Council of Genesis— decide and choose. But these beings can decide against God: is this not for Him the risk of destroying His creation? This risk, it is necessary to reply, must, paradoxically, register its presence at the very height of omnipotence. Creation, truly to "innovate," creates "the other," that is to say, a personal being capable of refusing Him Who created him. The peak of all-powerfulness is thus received as a powerlessness of God, as a divine risk. The person is the highest creation of God only because God gives it the possibility of love, therefore of refusal. God risks the eternal ruin of His highest creation, precisely that it may be the highest. The paradox is irreducible: in his very greatness, which is to be able to become God, man is fallible; but without fallibility there would be no greatness. That is why, confirm the Fathers, man must undergo a test, the πεῖρα, so as to gain awareness of his freedom, of the free love that God awaits from him.

"God created man like an animal who has received the order to become God," says a deep saying of St. Basil, reported by St. Gregory of Nazianzus. To execute this order, one must be able to refuse it. God becomes *powerless* before human freedom; He cannot violate it since it flows from His own omnipotence. Certainly man was created by the will of God alone; but he cannot be deified by it alone. A single will for creation, but two for deification. A single will to raise up the image, but two to make the image into a likeness. The love of God for man is so great that it cannot constrain; for there is no love without respect. *Divine will* always will submit itself to gropings, to detours, even to revolts of *human will* to bring it to a free consent: of such is divine providence, and the classical image of the pedagogue must seem feeble indeed to anyone who has felt God as a beggar of love waiting at the soul's door without ever daring to force it.

VI. Christian Anthropology

St. Maximus the Confessor has described with an incomparable power and fullness the mission devolving upon man. To the successive divisions that constitute creation there must correspond unions or syntheses accomplished by man, thanks to the "synergy" of freedom and grace.

The fundamental division in which the very reality of the created being is rooted is that of God and the assemblage of creatures, of the created and the uncreated. Created nature accordingly divides itself into celestial and terrestrial, into intelligible and sensible. In the sensible universe, heaven is separated from the earth. On the latter's surface, Paradise is set apart. Finally, the inhabitant of Paradise, man, is himself divided into two sexes, male and female.

Adam must overcome these divisions by a conscious action to reunite in himself the whole of the created cosmos and to become deified with it. He must first overcome the sexual separation by a chaste life, by a union more total than the external union of the sexes, by an "integrity" which would be integration. At a second stage, he must reunite Paradise to the rest of the terrestrial cosmos, by a love of God which would at once detach him from everything and allow him to embrace everything: always carrying Paradise in himself, he would have transformed the whole earth into Paradise. In the third place, his spirit, and his body itself, would triumph over space by unifying all of the sensible world, the earth and its firmament. At the next stage, he must penetrate into the celestial cosmos, live like the angels, assimilate their intelligence and reunite in himself the intelligible world to the sensible world. Finally, the cosmic Adam, by giving himself without return to God, would give Him back all His creation, and would receive from Him, by the mutuality of love, that is to say by grace, all that God possesses by virtue of His nature. Thus in the overcoming of the primordial separation of the created and uncreated, there would be accomplished man's deification, and by him, of the whole universe.

The Fall has rendered man inferior to his vocation. But

the divine plan has not changed. The mission of the first Adam accordingly must be fulfilled by the celestial Adam, namely Christ: not that He substitutes Himself for man, for the infinite love of God would not replace the bond of human freedom, but in order to return to man the possibility of accomplishing his task, to reopen for him the path to deification, this supreme synthesis, through man, of God and the created cosmos, wherein rests the meaning of all of Christian anthropology. Thus, because of sin, in order that man might become God, it was necessary that God should become man, and that the second Adam should inaugurate the "new creation" in surmounting all the divisions of the old one. Indeed by His virginal birth, Christ overcomes the division of the sexes and, for the redemption of "eros," opens two paths, united only in the person of Mary, at once virgin and mother: the path of Christian marriage and the path of monachism. On the cross Christ reunited the whole of the terrestrial cosmos to Paradise: for when He allowed death to enter Him to consume it by contact with His divinity, the darkest place on earth becomes radiant; there is no longer any accursed place. After the Resurrection, the very body of Christ mocks spatial limitations, and in an integration of all that is sensible, unifies earth and heaven. By the Ascension, Christ reunites the celestial and terrestrial worlds, the angelic choirs to the human race. Finally, He Who sits at the right hand of the Father introduces humanity above the angelic orders and into the Trinity Itself; and these are the first fruits of cosmic deification.

Thus we cannot rediscover the fullness of Adamic nature except in Christ, the second Adam. But to understand this nature better, we must pose two difficult, though, as it happens, connected problems: the problem of sex and that of death. Is the biological condition in which we find ourselves today that of man before the Fall? Is this condition, connected to the tragic dialectic of love and death, rooted in the paradisiacal state? Here the thought of the Fathers, precisely because it cannot evoke the earth-paradise except through the accursed earth, risks becoming incomplete, and thus opening itself to non-Christian influences which would make it partial. A dilemma emerges: either a biological sexuality exists in Paradise, as the divine order to multiply suggests. But then is this not, in man's first condition, a weakening of the divine image by the presence of an animality at once implying multiplicity and death? Or the paradisiacal condition is pure of all animality. But then sin exists in the very fact of our biological life, and we fall into a sort of Manichaeism.

Certainly the Fathers have rejected, with Origenism, this second solution. But they have succeeded only with difficulty in clarifying the first. Starting with the undeniable connection, in the fallen world, of sex and death, of animality and mortality, they ask themselves whether the creation of woman, raising up a biological condition linked to finitude, would not have threatened from the beginning of Paradise the potential immortality of man. Since this negative side of the division of the sexes introduces a certain fallibility, human nature would henceforth be vulnerable and the Fall inevitable.

Gregory of Nyssa, taken up on this point by Maximus the Confessor, has challenged this necessary linking of the sexual division and the Fall. For him, sexuality must have been created by God in prevision of sin, to preserve humanity after the Fall, though simply as a possibility. The sexual polarization endowed human nature with a safeguard that implies no constraint: likewise the passenger who is given a life-buoy, but is in no way tempted by this to hurl himself into the sea. This possibility can only be actualized at the moment when, through a sin that has nothing to do with sex, human nature will break and become closed to grace. It is only in this fallen state, in which death is the wages of sin, that possibility will become necessity. Here intervenes the exegesis, dating from Philo, of the "tunics of skin" with which God clothes man after the Fall: these tunics would represent our actual nature, our crude biological state, quite different from the transparent corporeality of Paradise. A new cosmos is formed, which defends itself against finitude through sex, thus founding the law of births and deaths. In this context, sex appears not as the cause of mortality, but as its relative antidote.

One cannot, however, follow Gregory when, arguing about this "preventive" character of sexuality, he affirms that the division into male and female is "super-imposed" upon the image. It is in fact not this division only, but all the divisions of creation which have acquired, in consequence of sin, a character of death and of separation. And human love, the absolute passion of lovers, has never ceased harbouring, in the very fatality of its failure, a paradisiacal nostalgia where heroism and art are rooted. Paradisiacal sexuality, stemming completely from consubstantial interiority and whose marvelous multiplication, which should fill everything, would certainly have demanded neither multiplicity nor death, is almost entirely unknown to us; for sin, by objectifying bodies ("they saw that they were naked"), made the first two human persons two separate natures, two individual beings, having between them external relations. But the new creation in Christ, the second Adam, allows us to perceive the profound meaning of a division which certainly had nothing "super-imposed": Mariology, the love of Christ and the Church, and the sacrament of marriage bring to light a fullness that originates in the creation of woman—fullness not glimpsed, however, except in the unique person of the Virgin, for our fallen condition always endures, demanding for the accomplishing of our human vocation not only the integrating chastity of marriage but also, and perhaps primarily, the sublimating chastity of monachism

Can one say that Adam, in his paradisiacal condition, was really immortal? "God did not create death," says the Book of Wisdom. For archaic theology—St. Irenaeus for example—Adam was neither necessarily mortal nor necessarily immortal: his nature, rich in possibilities, malleable, could be constantly nourished by grace and transformed by it to the point of surmounting all the risks of aging and death. The possibilities of mortality existed but in order to be made impossible. Such was the test of Adam's freedom. The tree of life at the center of Paradise and its nourishing of immortality offered therefore a possibility: thus, in our Christo-ecclesiastical realities, the Eucharist, which heals us, nourishes and fortifies us, spiritually and bodily. One must feed oneself with God to attain freely deification. And it is in this personal effort that Adam failed.

As for the divine interdiction, it poses a double problem: that of the knowledge of good and evil, and that of the interdict itself. Neither knowledge in itself, nor that of good and evil, is bad. But recourse to this discernment implies an existential inferiority, a fallen state. In the condition of sin, one must certainly know good and evil to do one and avoid the other. But for Adam in Paradise this knowledge has no use. The very existence of evil implies a voluntary separation from God, a denial of God. As long as Adam remained united with God and fulfilled His will, as long as he nourished himself with His presence, such a distinction was of no use.

That is why the divine interdiction was less the knowing of good and evil (since evil did not exist, other than as a risk, that of Adam's transgression itself) than a deliberate test, designed to make conscious the freedom of the first man. Adam was to emerge from an infantile unawareness by agreeing, through love, to obey God. Not that the interdict was arbitrary: for the love of God, if it was freely consented to by man, would engulf him completely, and through him make the universe transparent to grace. How then could he desire something else, isolate one aspect, one fruit, of this transparent universe to muddy it in egocentric desire, and with the same movement make it opaque and make himself opaque to the full divine presence? "Do not eat..." "Do not touch...": it is the very possibility of a really conscious love, of an ever-growing love that would take man away from an autonomous enjoyment not of one tree, but of all trees, not of one fruit, but of all that is sensible, to consume him, and all the universe with him, in enjoyment of God alone.

Chapter Three

ORIGINAL SIN

I. Introduction

The problem of evil is essentially Christian. For a clear-minded atheist, evil is only an aspect of the absurd. For a blind atheist, it is the temporary result of a still imperfect organization of society and the universe. In a monist metaphysic, it necessarily qualifies the created as separate from God; but it is then only an illusion. In a dualist metaphysic, it is still the "other," material or principial badness, but as eternal as God. Evil as a problem thus stems necessarily from Christianity. How then to explain it in a world created by God, in a vision in which creation appears intrinsically good? Even considering human liberty as opposing the divine plan, one cannot refrain from the question: what is evil?

Yet the question is badly put, for it implies that evil is "something." To hear it, one is tempted to see in evil an essence, the "principle of evil," the "anti-God" of the Manichaeans. The universe then appears a "no man's land" between the good God and the bad God, its richness and diversity as a play of light and shade, stemming from the struggle of these two principles.

This vision finds a certain basis in ascetic experience, and dualist elements have constantly tried to insinuate themselves into Christianity, particularly in monastic life. Yet for Orthodox thought, this vision is false: God has no counterpart, one cannot imagine natures that would be foreign to Him. From the end of the third century to St. Augustine, the Fathers have vigorously fought Manichaeism, but they have done so by using philosophical elements whose very problematic somewhat missed the question. For the Fathers in effect, evil is a lack, a vice, an imperfection: not a nature, but what a nature lacks to be perfect. In essentialist fashion, they think that evil does not exist, that it is only an inadequacy of being. This was answer enough to Manichaeism, but helpless before the reality of evil which we all feel, before the evil present and acting in the world. For finally, if the last request in the "Our Father" can be translated philosophically by "Deliver us from evil," the cry of our concrete anguish is certainly: "Deliver us from the evil-doer."

As Father Bouyer has pointedly noticed, the problem of evil, in an authentically Christian perspective, is reduced to that of the evil-doer. And the evil-doer is not an inadequacy of being, a lack of essentiality, no more indeed than he is, as an evil-doer, an essence; for his nature, created by God, is good. The evil-doer is a person, someone.

Evil certainly has no place among the essences, but it is not only a lack: there is an activity in it. Evil is not a nature, but a state of nature, as the Fathers would say most profoundly. It thus appears as an illness, as a parasite existing only by virtue of the nature he lives off. More precisely, it is a state of the will of this nature; it is a fallen will with regard to God. Evil is revolt against God, that is to say, a personal attitude. The exact vision of evil is thus not essentialist but personalist. "The word is placed in evil," says St. John: that is the state in which one finds the nature of those personal beings who have turned from God.

Thus the origin of evil lives in the liberty of creatures. That is why evil is inexcusable: for it has no other origin than the liberty of the being who accomplishes it. "There is no evil, or rather it exists only at the moment that it is done," writes Diadochus of Photice, and Gregory of Nyssa underlines the paradox of him who submits to evil: he exists in non-existence.

Man has thus given a place to evil in his will, and has introduced it into the world. Certainly man, who was naturally predisposed to know and love God, has chosen evil because it was suggested to him: that is exactly the serpent's role. Evil in man, and through man in the earthly cosmos, thus appears linked to a contamination: but the latter is not at all automatic; it could not be propagated except through a free acquiescence of human will. Man has agreed to allow himself to be dominated.

Yet evil has its origin in the angelic worlds and it is worth pausing here.

The angels cannot be defined as "incorporeal spirits." Even though called this by the Fathers and the liturgy, they are not "pure spirits." There is an angelic corporeality that can even make itself visible. Although the idea of the incorporeality of angels in the West ended by carrying the day with Thomism, the medieval Franciscans, notably Bonaventura, held to the opposite position. And in nineteenth-century Russia, Ignatius Brianchaninov defended this angelic corporeality against Theophanes the Recluse. Whatever the case, angels do not have a biological condition similar to ours, and know neither mortality nor reproduction. They have no "tunics of skin."

The unity of the angelic world is therefore completely different from ours. One may speak of the "human species," that is to say of countless persons possessing the same nature. But the angels, who are also persons, have no unity of nature. Each is a nature, an intelligible universe. Their unity is thus inorganic and, one may say by analogy, abstract: that of the city, the choir, the army, unity of service, of function, of praise, in sum, unity of harmony. In this way one may establish remarkable similarities between music and mathematics on one side, and angelic worlds on the other.

The angelic universe would therefore offer to evil other conditions than ours. The evil gathered by Adam could contaminate the whole of human nature. But the malefic attitude of an angel remains personal: here evil in some way is individualized. If there is contagion, it is by example, by the influence one person can exert on others. Thus Lucifer tempted other angels, but not all fell: the serpent overthrew a third of the stars, says the Apocalypse symbolically.

Evil originates therefore in the spiritual sin of the angel. And the attitude of Lucifer reveals to us the root of every sin: pride as revolt against God. He who was first called to deification by grace wished to be God by himself. The root of sin is thus the thirst for self-deification, the hatred of grace. Remaining dependent on God in his very being, since his being was created by God, the spirit in revolt consequently acquires a hatred of being, a frenzy to destroy, a thirst for an impossible nothingness. As only the earthly world remains open to him, he tries here to destroy the divine plan, and having failed to annihilate creation, to disfigure it. The drama that began in heaven continues on earth, as the faithful angels close the gates of heaven unyieldingly to the fallen angels.

The serpent in Genesis is Satan, as is also the "ancient dragon" of the Apocalypse. He is present in the earthly Paradise precisely because man must undergo the πεῖρα, the test of liberty. The first commandment, that of not touching the tree, locates human freedom, and it is following the same order of ideas that God permits the serpent's presence. "Faith makes sin live," it manifests it, as St. Paul has stressed. God gives this first commandment and immediately Satan insinuates revolt. In fact the fruit was good in itself, but everything hinges on the personal relationship of man and God. And when Eve sees that the tree is beautiful, a value outside of God appears. "You will be like God," says the serpent. He does not altogether deceive man: for the latter is called to deification. But here "like" signifies an equality, through resentment, of him who stands up to God: autonomous god against God, god by himself, god of the earthly cosmos isolated from God.

Once the fruit is eaten, sin develops in several stages. When God calls Adam, the latter, far from crying out with horror and throwing himself before his creator, accuses the woman: "she, whom Thou hast placed near me," he avers. Man therefore refuses his responsibility, throws it onto the woman and finally on God Himself. Adam is here the first determinist. Man is not free, he lets it be understood; creation, therefore God, has led him to evil.

Since then, man has been in possession of evil. His nature having become detached from God, becomes non-natural, anti-natural. The human spirit, brutally overturned, receives the image of amorphous matter instead of reflecting eternity; the first hierarchy of the human being, open to grace but overturning it into the cosmos, is itself overturned. The spirit should live from God, the soul from the spirit, the body from the soul. But the spirit begins to live off the soul, nurturing itself upon non-divine values, such as the autonomous goodness and beauty that the serpent revealed to the woman by drawing her attention to the tree. In its turn, the soul lives off the body, passions are born. The body finally lives off the earthly universe, kills to eat and thus finds death.

Yet God, and here lies the whole mystery of the "tunics of skin," introduces a certain order at the very heart of disorder to avoid a total disintegration by evil. His beneficent will organises and preserves the universe; His punishment is pedagogy: better that man dies, that is to say, be excluded from the tree of life, than that his monstrous condition be made eternal. His finitude itself would make repentance well up within him, that is to say, the possibility of a new love. But the universe, thus safeguarded, is not for all that the true world; this order where death takes place remains a catastrophic order. "The earth is accursed because of man" and the very beauty of the cosmos becomes ambiguous.

The true world, the real nature are only affirmed by grace. That is why sin opens the drama of redemption. The second Adam will choose God exactly there, where the first had chosen himself: Satan will come to Christ after His baptism and will proffer Him the same temptation. But three times temptation will break against the united wills of God and man.

II. The meaning of the Old Testament

In Paradise, the accord of human liberty and grace could throw a luminous bridge over this "infinite distance" which, according to St. John of Damascus, separates the creature from the creator. Adam was directly called to deify himself. But after the Fall, two obstacles intervene to make this distance unbridgeable: sin itself, which makes human nature incapable of receiving grace, and death, the outcome of that fallenness which precipitates man into an anti-natural state where the will of man, contaminating the cosmos, gives to non-being a paradoxical and tragic reality. In this state man can no longer correspond to his vocation. But God's plan has not changed: He always desires that man should be united with Him and transfigure the whole earth.

The last and fully positive end of man thereupon implies a negative aspect: salvation. So that man may return freely to God, it is first necessary for Him to free him from his sinful and mortal state. This state demands redemption, which in the fullness of the divine plan appears accordingly not as an end but as a negative means. For one cannot be saved unless one is the helpless prey of evil. After the Fall, human history is a long shipwreck awaiting rescue: but the port of salvation is not the goal; it is the possibility for the shipwrecked to resume his journey whose sole goal is union with God.

Thus after losing the paradisiacal state, man, objectively, can no longer attain his final end. His attitude in his new state of non-being and death is a painful passivity, based first on a tenacious paradisiacal nostalgia, then upon an ever more conscious waiting for salvation. The falling movement continues, making the waiting more poignant but also giving rise either to a thousand ways to forget (or try to forget) death, that is to say, separation from God, or to the Luciferian will to find salvation alone, and to self-deify. But Angelism and Babelism will fail, and men will not cease waiting for someone to come to their rescue. The whole history of humanity will thus be that of salvation, where one may discern three periods.

The first is a long preparation for the Saviour's coming. It ranges from the Fall to the Annunciation: for "today is the beginning of our salvation" sings the office of the feast. During this period, Providence does not cease from taking account of the will of men, and consequently choosing its instruments.

The second period, from the Annunciation to Pentecost, corresponds to the terrestrial life and Ascension of Christ.

Here man can do nothing: Christ alone, by His life, His Resurrection and His Ascension, accomplishes the work of salvation. In His person, humanity and divinity unite, eternity enters into time, time penetrates into eternity, the deified anthropocosmic nature is introduced into the divine life, at the very heart of the Trinity.

Then, with Pentecost, begins a new period when human persons, supported by the Holy Spirit, must freely acquire this deification that their nature has received, once and for all, in Christ. In the Church liberty and grace collaborate. Through respect for human liberty, God allows the age of sin and of death to continue; for He does not want to impose Himself on man. He wants the answer of faith and love. Yet our situation is incomparably superior to the paradisiacal state: in fact we no longer risk losing grace; we can always participate in the theandric fullness of the Church. Through penitence and faith, the very conditions of our Fall, assumed to their depths by Christ, open to the mystery of love. The history of the Church is therefore a free and conscious grasping by men, of the unity realized in Christ and ever present in the Church where the eternal splendour of the kingdom is already given to us. Thus we collaborate in the definitive abolition of death and in the cosmic transfiguration, that is to say, in the second coming of the Lord.

The period of preparation is that of the promise. It is a slow progression to Christ during which the divine "pedagogy" tries to make possible the fulfillment of the promise made at the very moment of punishment.

The Old Testament did not know the intimate sanctification by grace, yet it knew saintliness, for grace, from outside, aroused it in the soul as an effect. The man who submitted to God in faith and lived in all righteousness could become the instrument of His will. As is proved by the vocation of prophets, it is not a question of agreement between two wills, but of lordly utilization of the human will by that of God: the Spirit of God swoops upon the seer, God takes possession of man by imposing Himself from outside on his person. God, invisible, speaks: His servant listens. The darkness of Sinai is opposed to the light of Tabor like a veiled mystery to an unveiled mystery. Man prepares himself to serve in the obscurity of faith, by obedience and purity. Obedience and purity are negative concepts: they imply the exteriority of God and the instrumental submission of man who, even when just, cannot free himself from his state of sin and death. Saintliness, as active sanctification of all being and the free assimilation of human nature to that of God, can only manifest itself after the work of Christ, by the conscious grasping of this work. That is why the Law is essential to the Old Testament, and the relationship of man and God is not union but alliance, guaranteed by loyalty to the Law.

The history of the Old Testament is that of elections linked to successive falls. Through these God saves a "remnant" whose patient waiting purifies: through the very dialectic of disappointments, the awaiting of the triumphal Messiah becomes that of the Suffering Servant of Yahweh, the awaiting of the political liberation of a people, that of the spiritual liberation of humanity. The more God recedes, the more man's prayer deepens; the more the election is limited, the more its goal is universalized: until the supreme purity of the Virgin is capable of giving birth to the Saviour of humanity.

The first fall, after the loss of Paradise, was the murder of Abel by Cain. Yet God had said to Cain: "Is sin not lying at your door? Its desire reaches you; you must dominate it" (Gen. 4:7). But Cain killed his brother. To this first fall corresponded a first election: that of Seth and his progeny. The sons of Seth are "the sons of God": they invoke the name of Yahweh and one of them, Enoch, "walked with God" and was perhaps carried with his body into Paradise. The descendants of Cain, on the other hand, are only the sons of man, tragically delivered to death ("I killed a man for my wound and a young man for my bruise," says Lamech). Cursed by the cultivated earth whose mouth must have drunk Abel's blood, they are the first citizens, the inventors of arts and techniques. With them, civilization appears, immense compensation for the absence of God! One must forget God or replace Him: forget Him by forging metals, by allowing oneself to be captivated by the weight of the earth and the opaque power it confers: thus Tubal-Cain, "the blacksmith, father of all craftsmen in bronze and iron" (Gen. 4:22); replace Him by the feast of art, by the nostalgic consolation of music: thus Jubal, "father of all those who play the lyre and the pipe." The arts here appear as cultural, not cult, values; they are a prayer that is lost since it is not addressed to God. The beauty they raise up closes back on itself to enchain man with its magic. These inventions inaugurate culture as the cult of an abstraction, empty of that Presence to which every cult must be addressed...

Then came the Flood, and God seems to allow His creation, ravaged by corruption, to return to the original waters. Perhaps one must connect this new fall to the mysterious commerce of angels and men (Gen. 6:1-4), whence resulted the appearance of "giants": was this not a Luciferian gnosis whence man drew prodigious powers? Whatever the case, a remnant, a man and his family, found grace in the eyes of God: "for Noah was a just man, honest among the men of his time, Noah walked with God" (Gen. 6:9). Noah saved humanity and all the earthly creatures, not by regenerating them as does Christ of Whom he is only the prototype, but by assuring their continuity. After the Flood, God concluded a cosmic alliance with humanity which stabilizes the earthly universe and takes the rainbow for a sign, that mysterious bridge of light that links earth and heaven.

But a new fall intervenes with the construction of Babel. Babel signifies the usurping movement of a civilization without God, a purely human unity, entirely created from earth in the desire to conquer heaven. Thus the sacerdotal civilizations of the Orient raised their ziggurats, those temples whose storeys without doubt symbolized the ladder of interiority that the initiated must methodically ascend. Babel typifies and goes beyond these archaic examples, and remains ever-present.

Unity without God brought dispersion far from God as a just punishment. Then was born the diversity of tongues, the chaos of "nations." But God uses evil itself to reply to the fall through election: in those peoples who gather at the heart of this disunion and intermingling, He chose one as an instrument; among the descendants of Shem, Eber gave his name to the Hebrews. This election culminates in the alliance of Abraham, a historical election this time, where the glory of a progeny more in number than the stars in heaven is announced. But Abraham must be tested in his very hope so that it might be fully confirmed. The sacrifice asked of him, that of Isaac, the inheritor of the promise, demands a faith beyond all logic, an unconditional obedience. Abraham says to Isaac who questions him, as they climb Moriah: "God will see and find a lamb for this burnt-offering, my son"; and when God, at the last moment, in fact replaces the human victim with a ram, one understands that He is preparing the divine Lamb, Christ, every time man obeys. How could He not give His own Son when man has given his? Thus the history of the Old Testament is not only that of the foreshadowings of salvation but that of man's refusals and acceptances. Salvation approaches or withdraws as man prepares or not to receive it. The καιρὸς of Christ, His moment, will depend on human will. The entire meaning of the Old Testament lies in these fluctuations underlining the double aspect of Providence. The latter is not unilateral. It takes into account the human waiting and call. Divine pedagogy scrutinizes man, tests his dispositions.

This testing is sometimes a struggle, for God wishes that human liberty should not only resist Him but force Him, if not to reveal His name, at least to bless: thus Jacob becomes Israel "for you have wrestled with God and with man and you have won" (Gen. 32:29). And the patriarch *becomes* the people, and when this people is captive in Egypt, God raises up Moses to deliver it. On Sinai, God passes in His glory before Moses but prevents him seeing His Face "for man cannot see Me and live": divine nature remains hidden. But the election of Israel, the decisive stage, is affirmed in a new alliance: that of the Law. A written obligation to which the chosen people must submit, the Law is accompanied by divine promises that the Prophets will continue to make precise. Thus the Law and the Prophets complement each other; and Christ will always evoke them together to underline their completeness. The Prophets are the men whom

God chose to announce the profound meaning of His Law. In contrast to the Pharisees, who gradually turned the Law into a static reality and the means of justification, the Prophets explain its spirit, its historical dynamism, the eschatological call that it contains in making man take cognizance of his sin and his helplessness before it.

The Prophets, in their relationship to the chosen people, therefore play an analogous role to that of Tradition in the Church: Prophets and Tradition in fact show us the real meaning of the Scriptures. And the duality of Law-Prophets already expresses *aliquo modo* the defining action of the Logos and the life-giving action of the Holy Spirit. In the Old Testament in fact the spirit of prophecy makes us perceive clearly the action of the third person of the Trinity.

The elections slowly tighten up: in Israel the tribe of Judah, in Judah the house of David. Thus grows the tree of Jesse until the supreme election of the Virgin. This election was announced to Mary by the angel Gabriel. But Mary remained free to accept or to refuse. The whole history of the world, every fulfillment of the divine plan, was dependent on this free human response. The humble consent of the Virgin allowed the Word to become flesh.

"Behold the handmaiden of the Lord: be it unto me according to Thy Word" (Luke 1:38). Everything God had waited for from fallen humanity was realized in Mary: a personal liberty finally opened her flesh, her human nature, to the necessary work of salvation. The second person of the Trinity could enter into history, not by a brutal irruption in which man would remain an instrument, not by a setting aside of the Virgin, separated from the progeny of Adam, but by a consent in which the enduring divine pedagogy finally found its reward. This is because God had involved Himself, with all the seriousness and respect of love, in the history of man's salvation in order that the Virgin, epitomizing all the saintliness of the Old Testament, might offer to this love the pure abode of her flesh. Her ancestors, blessed by God and purified by the Law, spiritually received the words of the Word. She could bodily receive the Word Himself. By giving birth to a divine person who borrows His humanity from her, she really becomes the Mother of God. That is why St. John of Damascus could write: "The name of the Mother of God (Θεοτόκος) contains the whole history of divine economy in the world." But the saintliness of the Old Testament did not only give to the Word His mother, and, one could say, His Bride: it prophetically destined her for Israel. Mary is the silence that incarnates. The Baptist, in the spirit of Elijah, is the voice that cries in the wilderness: the last prophet, he recognized and pointed to "the Lamb Who took upon Himself the sins of the world." The Old Testament culminates in these two beings whom iconography exalts on either side of Christ in glory: the Bride and the Friend of the Bridegroom.

III. The Incarnation

In verse 14 of St. John's Prologue, which concerns both Christ and the Trinity, resounds the great Christian certainty, the very same one that the young Augustine vainly searched for in Plotinus's metaphysic: "the Word is become flesh." As St. John emphasizes, all that we know of the Trinity we know through the Incarnation. Revelation is consummated when a divine person, that of the Son of God, becomes Son of man and "lives among us." Certainly, non-Christian thought has often had presentiments of the mystery of the number three, but through the obscurity of ambiguous symbols, and the full revelation of the Trinity demanded the Incarnation. Ever since then the Old Testament is revealed as trinitarian, the master of the universe appears as Father, and man, contemplating "the glory that an only Son holds from His Father," sees the divine nature opening itself: theology as contemplation of God Himself becomes possible: ὁ λόγος σὰρξ ἐγένετο, "the Word is become flesh." Then begins the economy proper to the Son Who enters into the history of the world. "The flesh" in effect is the final limit of inhumanation: not only the soul but the body is assumed by the Word. It is the totality of human nature that is meant here by the word "flesh." And the "becoming" of the Word "becoming flesh" is added to the fullness of the divine being, to the great scandal of metaphysics. The Son remains God at the heart of the unchanged Trinity. But something is added to His divinity: He becomes man. An incomprehensible paradox: the Word, without a change in His divine nature, which nothing can diminish, fully engages in our condition to the point of accepting even death. A supreme manifestation of love, this mystery cannot be broached except in terms of personal life: for the person of the Son overcomes the frontiers of the transcendent and the immanent and can become engaged in human history. This "becoming" goes beyond the categories of divine nature, eternal, unchangeable, but with which the hypostases do not identify: that is why Christ becomes man without the other persons of the Trinity suffering or being crucified, and that is why one must speak of the economy proper to the Son. Certainly economy belongs to the divine will and this is unique to the Trinity; certainly the salvation of the world is the single will of the Three, "and he who is initiated into the mystery of the Resurrection, learns the end for which God created all things in the beginning" (St. Maximus the Confessor). But this common will is realized differently for each person: the Father sends, the Son obeys, the Spirit accompanies and helps and through It the Son enters the world. The will of the Son is that of the Trinity, but it is rather obedience. It is the Trinity that saves us, but it is the Son Who is incarnated to realize in the world the work of salvation. For the Patripassians, the Father suffered, the Father was crucified with the Son because of the unity of nature. This was to confound in God nature and person. But we strongly feel that if our distinctions are to avoid heresy, they cannot do more than encircle the mystery: paths rigorously blazed through faith and prayer, they are only words without them. The mystery here is that of obedience. For in God all is unity. But in Christ, there was not only divine will, but human will, and since a separation was introduced between the Son and the Father, the accord of the two wills in Christ seals the obedience of the Son to the Father; and the mystery of this obedience is one and the same as that of our salvation.

The Son is incarnated to make possible the union of man with God, a union not only interrupted, but forbidden without human recourse to evil. The mere fact of incarnation overcomes the first obstacle to this union: the separation of the two natures, that of man and that of God. Two other obstacles then remain, linked to the fallen condition of man: sin and death. The work of Christ is to vanquish them, to banish their necessity from the terrestrial cosmos. Not to overcome them without redress, for that would be to violate the very liberty that created them. But to make death harmless and sin curable by submission of God Himself to death and hell. Thus the death of Christ removes, from between man and God, the obstacle of sin; and His Resurrection takes from death its "sting." God descends to the meonic abysses, opened in creation by Adam's sin, so that man might ascend to divinity. "God has become man in order that man might become God": the sentence occurs three times in St. Irenaeus, one finds it again in St. Athanasius, and it ends by becoming an adage common to theologians of all ages. St. Peter was the first to write: We must "become partakers of the divine nature" (II Peter 1:4). The profound meaning of the Incarnation resides in this physical and metaphysical vision of nature metamorphosized by grace, in this restoration henceforth acquired by human nature, in this breach opened through the opaqueness of death that leads to deification.

"The first man, Adam, became a living soul. The second Adam became a life-giving spirit. . . . The first man, being wrenched from the soil, is made of dust; the second comes from heaven. As was the man of dust, just so are those who are of dust; and as was the celestial man, just so are those who are celestial. And just as we have carried the likeness of the man of dust, so also shall we carry the likeness of the man who is celestial" (I Cor. 15:45-49). Christ is therefore the new Adam come from heaven, the second and last man. Would not this "celestial man" be the manifestation on our earth of another humanity, of a superior humanity in the heavens, as certain gnostics have thought? But where then would be the Incarnation? For Christ would pass through His mother without taking anything from her. For the mystery of the Incarnation is that of the God-man, Who truly reunites the two natures and takes from the Virgin His humanity. The miracle of humanity is this: that the Word accepts from His own creature; God solicits from Mary at the decisive moment of the Annunciation the first-fruits of His humanity, His own human nature.

The Incarnation was effected by the action of the Holy Spirit. Is this to say, as certain theologians have claimed, that the Spirit is the spouse of the Virgin, that It corresponds to the role of spouse in the Immaculate Conception? That would be grossly to rationalize the birth of Christ. For if one can talk of "husband" in the case of the Virgin, it is only in a metaphorical manner: in the degree that she represents the Church, she has no other husband than her Son. In this conception without seed, the seed is the Word Himself. And the Spirit, far from being the husband of Mary, completes the purification of her heart, *makes her fully virgin, and also confers on her through the very fullness of integrity, the strength to gather and give birth to the Word: the most total virginity, which the Spirit confers as a purity of the whole being, coincides with divine maternity.*

Thus there is no human person in Christ: there is humanity, but the person is divine. Christ is man but His person comes from heaven. Whence the Pauline expression "celestial man."

Can one speak of the union of two natures, of their "concourse" as the Fathers called it? The Fathers themselves were always refining their language and constraining us to purify ours. The humanity of Christ has never constituted a distinct and anterior nature; it has not come to unite itself with divinity. It never existed outside of the person of Christ; it is He Who has created it from the center of His hypostasis, not *ex nihilo,* since it is necessary to redeem all of history, the total human condition, starting with the Virgin, purified by the Holy Spirit. The uncreated person Himself creates His human nature, and the latter appears from the start as the humanity of the Word. Strictly speaking, it is not a question of union nor even of assumption, but of the unity of two natures in the person of the Word from the moment of His incarnation. "The unlimited one," writes St. Maximus, "is limited in an effable fashion, whilst the limited one opens himself up to the measure of the unlimited one." God enters flesh into the flesh of history: history is risk; God runs a risk. He, completeness and plenitude itself, descends unto the last confines of the being which sin riddles with incompleteness and implenitude, to make salvation possible to free beings without shattering their freedom.

Chapter Four

CHRISTOLOGICAL DOGMA

I. Introduction

The Trinity is present in the very intellectual structure of christological dogma, that is, in the distinction between person and nature. The Trinity is one nature in three persons; Christ is a single person in two natures. Divinity and humanity, however separated they may appear by that infinite chasm which yawns between created and uncreated, are reconciled in the unity of one person.

Between triadology and christology there is a link, *consubstantiality:* for the term *homoousios,* meant originally to clarify the unity of Father and Son within the Trinity, is found again in the christological dogma definitively formulated at Chalcedon. On the one hand, Christ is consubstantial with the Father by His divinity. On the other, He is consubstantial with us by His humanity. There are therefore two consubstantialities, but a single real presence, a single person, at once true God and true man. The hypostasis encapsulates two natures. It remains one while becoming the other, without divinity being transformed into humanity, nor humanity into divinity.

The dogma of Chalcedon, which clarified this christological mystery of the two in one, is the culmination of a long fight against the temptation to rationalize the Incarnation by conjuring away either the divinity or the humanity of Christ. In the background, in other words, stand silhouetted the two great theological opponents of Christian antiquity: the schools of Alexandria and Antioch. The school of Antioch was a school of literal exegesis, which concentrated mostly on the historical side of the Scriptures. Every symbolic interpretation, every gnosis of the sacred event, seemed suspect to it, and the presence of the eternal in history escaped it time and again. Jesus thus risked appearing as one individual in the history of Judaea, in a history all too human in its temporal setting. At Antioch, history became insular often to the point of neglecting the magnificent vision of God become man. Opposed to this, the school of Alexandria, centering upon Christian gnosis, often emptied the biblical event of its concrete simplicity through an exegesis overgiven to allegory, and tended to depreciate the historical aspect, the human aspect of the Incarnation. These two schools gave rise to great theologians, but also to great heretics, whenever each succumbed to the temptation peculiar to it.

Issuing from Antiochian thought, Nestorianism dissected Christ into two different persons. Each consubstantiality giving rise to a single consubstantial being, two consubstantials have appeared: the Son of God and the Son of man, separated so far as they are persons. In truth, terminology was not yet settled, the distinction between persons and nature remaining confused; and the thought of Nestorius was for a long time able to lead astray. This Patriarch of Constantinople belonged to the school of Antioch, where he had great theologians for masters, some, like Theodore of Mopsuestia, clearly tending to heresy. (Theodore was condemned *post mortem* in the sixth century by the Fifth Ecumenical Council.) Nestorius carefully distinguished between the two natures, and his construction seemed orthodox until he denied the title of Mother of God, "Theotokos," to the Virgin, and tried to replace it by that of "Christotokos." This enraged the piety of the simple believer, and Nestorius had caused a scandal. For not being able to grasp the mystery of personhood, he now conceived the person in terms of nature, and finally identified the first with the second. He accordingly opposed the person of the Word to that of Jesus, though they were certainly united—but by a moral connection, by an election that made Jesus the receptacle of the Word. For Nestorius, only the human person of Christ was born from the Virgin; consequently, she was mother of Christ, but not of God. The two sons, of God and of man, were united but not one in Christ.

And yet, if Christ has no unity of person, our nature is not authentically assumed by God and the Incarnation ceases to be a "physical" restoration. If there is no real unity in Christ, a union between man and God is no longer possible. The whole doctrine of salvation loses its ontological foundation. We remain separated from God. Deification is forbidden; Christ is no more than a great exemplar; and Christianity becomes morality, an imitation of Jesus.

The single-minded opposition of Eastern piety rapidly evicted Nestorianism, but its very violence engendered the opposite heresy. To defend the unity of Christ, they expressed it in terms of nature, and of divine nature through respect for the Word. St. Cyril of Alexandria, in his polemic against Nestorius, launched the formula: a single nature in the Word incarnate. With him it was a simple fault of vocabulary, as the context shows. St. Cyril remains orthodox. But certain of his disciples followed the formula to the letter: a single nature in Christ, His divinity. Whence the very name of this heresy: Monophysitism (from μόνη, single, and φύσις, nature). The Monophysites did not deny the humanity of Christ as such, yet it did seem to them to be drowned in His divinity, like a drop of wine in the ocean. Humanity, dissolved in divinity, or volatilized in contact with it, as a little water thrown into a brazier. "The Word became flesh," the Monophysites constantly repeat; but to them, this "became" is that of water becoming ice: an appearance, a likeness, for all is divine in Christ. Thus Christ is consubstantial with the Father, but not with man. He passed through the Virgin without borrowing anything from her; He merely used her to make His appearance.

However many their nuances, there is no denying that one point remained ever-constant among the Monophysites: Christ is really God, but not really man. At the limit, the humanity of Christ is only an appearance, and Monophysitism ends in Docetism.

Nestorianism and Monophysitism—both are manifestations within the church of two pre-Christian tendencies which have not stopped threatening Christianity since: on one hand, the humanism of the West, the legacy of Athens and Rome; on the other hand, the cosmic illusionism and pure interiority of the ancient East, with its Absolute in which everything is reabsorbed (the image of water and ice is classical in India to illustrate the relation of finite and infinite). On one side, the human closes in upon itself; on the other it drowns itself in the divine. Between these two opposing temptations, the dogma of Chalcedon defines, around Christ true God and true man, the truth of God and of man, and the mystery of their unity without separation or absorption. "Conforming to the tradition of the Fathers, we proclaim in unanimity that one must confess a single and only Son, Our Lord Jesus Christ, perfect in divinity and perfect in humanity, true God and true man consubstantial with the Father by divinity and consubstantial with us by humanity, similar to us in everything, except sin, born of the Father before all ages according to divinity, born in these last times of Mary the Virgin, Mother of God, according to humanity, for us and for our salvation; a single and only Christ, Son, Lord, the Only-Begotten makes Himself known in two natures without mixture, without change, indivisibly, inseparably, in such a way that the union does not destroy the difference of the two natures, but on the contrary the properties of each only remain more firm when they are united in a single person or hypostasis which does not separate nor divide into two persons, being the same and single person of the Son, Monogene, God and Word, Lord Jesus Christ."

"Without mixture, without change, indivisibly, inseparably"—thus are united the two natures in the person of Christ. And of these terms, the first two were directed against the Monophysites and the last two against the Nestorians. In fact, the four definitions are negative: ἀσυγχύτως, ἀτρέπτως, ἀδιαιρέτως, ἀχωρίστως. They encompass, apophatically, the mystery of the Incarnation, but forbid us to imagine the "why." Christ is fully God: a little child in the cradle or agonizing on the cross, He does not cease from participating in trinitarian fullness, nor from governing the universe by His ever-present power. "O Christ, present in body in the tomb and in soul in Hell, as God Thou wast in Paradise with the thief and on the throne with the Father and the Spirit—Thou, the Infinite Who fillest all things," cries the Liturgy of St. John Chrysostom. For on the other hand, Christ's humanity is fully ours. It does not belong to Him by His eternal birth, but His divine person raised it in Mary. Christ thus has two wills, two intellects, two ways of acting, but always united in a single person. In each of His acts, there will be two energies in play: divine energy and human energy. It is thus puerile to construct a psychology of Christ, and in writing "the life of Christ" to reconstitute His "spiritual states." We cannot conjecture—and this is also the meaning of the four negations of Chalcedon—"how" the divine and the human coexisted in the same person. Even less, let us repeat, should one complain of the fact that Christ is not a "human person." His humanity does not have its own hypostasis, among the countless hypostases of men. Like us he has a body, like us a soul, like us a spirit, but our person is not this assemblage; it lives through and beyond the body, the soul, and the spirit which never constitute its nature. And while man, through his person, can leave the world, it is by his person that the Son of God can enter it; for His person, Whose nature is divine, "enhypostasizes" human nature, as Leontius of Byzantium said in the sixth century.

The two natures of Christ, without being mixed, nonetheless know a certain interpenetration. The divine energies radiate the divinity of Christ and penetrate His humanity: the latter is therefore deified from the moment of the Incarnation, like an iron in a brazier that becomes fire though remaining iron by nature. The Transfiguration partially reveals to the Apostles this blazing of divine energies irradiating the human nature of their Master. This interpenetration of two natures—at once penetration of divinity into flesh and the possibility henceforth acquired by it to penetrate into divinity—is called *perichoresis*— as St. Maximus the Confessor writes —or, in Latin, *communicatio idiomatum*. "The flesh became Word without losing what it had, while identifying with the Word according to the hypostasis," says St. John of Damascus. Christ becomes man by love while remaining God, and the fire of His divinity forever embraces human nature: that is why the saints, while remaining men, can participate in divinity and become God through grace.

II. "Form of God" and "Form of Servant"

"Have in you the very same sentiments that one must have in Christ. Though He was of divine form, He did not avail Himself of His equality with God; on the contrary, He divests Himself, taking the form of a slave and making Himself like men. Having thus put on the aspect of man, He lowered Himself yet more by making Himself obedient unto death, even death on the cross. That is why God has exalted Him supremely and given Him the Name which is above all names, so that at the name of Jesus every knee should bend, in the heavens, on earth, and in Hell, and so that every tongue should profess that Jesus Christ is Lord, to the glory of God the Father" (Phil. 2:5-11). This celebrated "kenotic" passage in the Epistle to the Philippians defines the exinanition of the Word: being in the "form of God," μορφὴ Θεοῦ, that is to say in the same condition as God, being of divine nature, He is emptied, divested, humiliated (ἐκένωσεν) in taking the condition of servant (μορφὴ δούλου). The Son of God, by a prodigious humbling, by the mystery of His kenosis (κένωσις), descends into a self-annihilating condition (not in the sense of the original nothing, but of the meonic gulf opened by the fallen state of man); paradoxically, He unites to the integral fullness of His divine nature the unfullness no less integral to fallen human nature.

This passage must be compared to the text of Isaiah on "the man of sorrows," on the prediction, so very scandalous to the Israelites, not of a Messiah arrayed in glory, but of a "servant of Yahweh," suffering and humiliated, giving Himself in silence as the "expiatory sacrifice," and "pierced for our transgressions" (Isaiah 53).

St. Cyril of Alexandria has examined this divine kenosis at length. God, he says, could not divest His nature in incarnating Himself, else He would no longer be God and one could no longer talk of the Incarnation. This means that the subject of kenosis is not divine nature, but the person of the Son. And the person fulfills himself in the gift of himself: he distinguishes himself from nature, not to "avail himself" of his natural condition, but to renounce himself totally. That is why the Son "did not avail Himself of His equality with God," but "on the contrary, divests Himself," *which is not a sudden decision, nor an act, but the manifestation of His very being, of personhood, which is no longer a willing of His own, but His very hypostatic reality as the expression of the trinitarian will, a will of which the Father is the source, the Son, the obedient realization, and the Spirit, the glorious fulfillment. There is therefore a profound continuity between the personal being of the Son as renunciation and His earthly kenosis.* Abandoning a glorious condition of which He never "availed Himself," He accepts shame, ignominy, accursedness. He assumes the objective conditions of sin. He submits to our mortal condition. Shedding His royal prerogatives, He hides His glory more and more, in suffering and death. For He must discover in His own flesh how far the man whom He created in His supremely beautiful image was made ugly by corruption.

Kenosis is therefore the Incarnation in its aspect of humility and death. But Christ zealously guards His divine nature and His exinanition is voluntary: though remaining God, He accepts becoming mortal, for the only way to conquer death was to allow it to penetrate God Himself where it could find no place.

Kenosis is the humbling of the servant who does not seek His own glory but that of the Father who sent Him. Christ never, or almost never, affirms His divinity. In renouncing Himself totally, in making His divine nature inconspicuous, in abandoning every will of His own to the point of saying: "the Father is greater than I," He accomplishes on earth the Trinity's work of love. And by the infinite respect that He witnesses towards human liberty, to the point of showing men only the sorrowful brotherly face of the slave and the sorrowful brotherly flesh of the cross, He awakens faith in man as a response to love: for only the eyes of faith recognize the form of God beneath the form of the slave and, deciphering beneath the human face the presence of a divine person, learn to unveil in each face the mystery of the person created in the image of God.

Yet before Christ's kenosis ends with His Resurrection, two theophanies were produced through His humanity: one at the Baptism, the other at the Transfiguration. Every time Christ manifested Himself not in His "form of slave" but in his "form of God," He let His divine nature, that is, His unity with the Father and the Spirit, shine through His deified humanity, for, according to St. Maximus the Confessor, His economically corruptible humanity was naturally incorruptible. The voice of the Father, the presence of the Holy Spirit in the form of a cloud or a dove, made these two manifestations of the "form of God" two trinitarian theophanies. The kontakion for the feast of the Transfiguration stresses that the disciples saw divine glory "according to their capacity" so that "when they see Thy crucifixion and death, they might understand that Thou didst freely submit to them" and not from any necessity of nature.

That this "light of the Transfiguration has no beginning and no end" (St. Gregory Palamas) should make us yet more aware of the reality of kenosis. Christ accepted, voluntarily and totally, the consequences of our sin, from the Incarnation unto death. He knew all the infirmities, all the humiliations of our condition, but not the destructive passions that depend on our liberty. And even the second Adam, to "conform" completely to the first, permitted the tempter to approach, not in Paradise this time, but in the condition of fallen man. Only in Christ did non-existence become suffering and love, and not evil or hate: that is why the tempter was rejected by Him Who bore in Himself more than Paradise, by Him Who is.

III. Two Energies, Two Wills

The definitions of Chalcedon are not directed only against

Nestorianism and Monophysitism, but, when they specify that Christ as perfect man is composed of a rational soul and of a body, against another heresy: Apollinarianism. Apollinarius of Laodicea lived in the fourth century, and the great Cappadocians fought against him. He was a typical representative of the school of Alexandria, where the unity of Christ was affirmed before all else. Eighty years before Monophysitism, and while its thought was still in preparation, he was asking how to reconcile this unity with the duality therein of the divine and the human. It could not be a matter, he thought, of two perfect natures, for according to Hellenistic thought, of which he was here a captive, "two perfects cannot become one," two perfect principles could not unite to form a third nature, also perfect. Either these two natures are not perfect, or their unity is only juxtaposition. In short, Apollinarius hypostasized the two natures, thereby refuting Nestorianism from the start, for it is quite obvious that two persons cannot cancel themselves into a third by their union. Since Christ's unity is perfect, one must therefore suppose that one of His constituents was not. Divinity here not being under attack, Apollinarius concluded that Christ's humanity, to make place for His divinity, must be imperfect. Man becomes perfect by intellect: it therefore seemed obvious to Apollinarius that Christ had no human νοῦς, and to seal His unity the human spirit in Him gave way to the divine Logos. The Word thus joins divinity to incomplete humanity, for divinity completed humanity. Thus the Christ of Apollinarius was less the God-man than an animal plus God. It was already the germ of Monophysitism, which will not cease to bring to the subject of the Christ the idea of incomplete humanity, thereby completed, and indeed absorbed, by the Logos.

In the last analysis the whole construction of Apollinarius is based on an identification of the human person and νοῦς: the great temptation for metaphysicians is thus to reduce the mystery of personhood to the best part of nature, the intellect, the one that is most familiar to them—and not without a disdainful note for sentiment and the body.

Chalcedon escaped the problem by distinguishing person and nature. This distinction, which established the liberty of personhood by contrast with the whole of nature, allows the affirmation of the unity of the two perfect principles, a unity that does not abolish but confirms "the properties of each nature." Human nature safeguards its fullness in Christ: it is not mutilated but fulfilled by the person who "enhypostasizes" it, and who is not here created but divine. The Logos does not replace an element of human nature: He is the person who assumes it in its totality.

Christ is therefore perfect man, at once body and rational soul. Here the word "rational" must be taken in the strong sense given it by the Fathers: "rational soul" is identified with νοῦς, with the intellect, and distinguishes itself from the animated body which can be divided into body and living soul. Thus the dichotomy of Chalcedon reaffirms the trichotomy, Pauline and traditional, of body, soul and spirit.

After Chalcedon there appeared new forms of Monophysitism which, while submitting to the letter of the symbol, sought to empty it of its content. This long effort to "dechalcedonize" Chalcedon was due either to the tenacious Monophysite instinct of Oriental spirituality, or to a search, of a mostly political order, for a compromise with the true Monophysites. The first motivation explains the doctrine of Monoenergism which developed at the end of the fifth century and the beginning of the sixth. Its supporters recognized two natures, but affirmed that their operation, that is to say the energy that manifests them, remains unique. The distinction of humanity and divinity is then no longer a mere abstraction: either the two natures are mixed, or humanity is entirely passive and divinity the sole agent.

This doctrine was refuted in the seventh century by several Fathers, in whose first rank stood St. Maximus the Confessor. One must conceive in Christ at once two distinct operations and a single goal, a single act, a single result. Christ acts through these two natures, as a sword reddened in the fire cuts and burns at the same time. Each nature cooperates in the single act according to the manner suitable to it: "It is not human nature that raised up Lazarus, it is not divine strength that wept before his tomb," writes St. John of Damascus.

Another form of compromise with Monophysitism, and

this time deliberate, was Monothelitism. It also admitted two natures, but a single will, the divine will, to which the human will conforms until it is swallowed up. The representatives of this doctrine were particularly clever politicians; as background to this compromise, the eastern provinces of the Empire were being eroded by Monophysitism on the one side, and the imperial desire for union on the other. Accordingly, three patriarchs—Cyril of Alexandria, Sergius of Constantinople and Honorius, Pope of Rome—found themselves engaged in fairly artificial elaboration of doctrine. Honorius, more or less pilloried by the other two, was, perhaps, alone sincere. He was, nonetheless, to be condemned as a heretic after his death by the Sixth Ecumenical Council.

St. Sophronius, Patriarch of Jerusalem, despite his advancing years, still found time before he died to enter protest. Following him, the successors of Honorius, Popes St. Martin and St. Agatho, took up the reaction. But the one who really saved the Church was a simple monk, already a great adversary of Monoenergism, Maximus the Confessor. He was exiled with St. Martin. The Pope died in exile. Maximus, brought back to Constantinople, still solemnly refused to adhere to the compromise the Church had appeared to adopt. "Even if the whole universe communed with you, I alone would not commune," he declared, strongly against the entire hierarchy yet witnessing to the truth. He was then cruelly mutilated and sent back into exile where he died. But his resistance saved the truth, which was not long in imposing itself upon the whole Church. It is therefore to oppose Monothelitism that we follow the argumentation of Maximus, where profound anthropological insights abound.

Monothelitism, like most of the heresies of this type, presupposed a definition of personhood in terms of one of its faculties. Here, it was the will that was attributed to the hypostasis. To elucidate the problem of two wills in Christ, St. Maximus starts from established triadological data. In the Trinity there are three persons and one nature; and the will is common to all three; there is only one will. The will thus is attached to the notion of nature and not of person: else one would have to posit three wills in the Trinity.

This transcendence of the person in relation to his will offends our usual conceptions, and this is because they concern only the individual, who certainly attributes the will to himself to affirm his own "ego". With a great show of finesse, St. Maximus here analyzes the concept of will. He distinguishes two sorts of will: the first, θέλησις φυσική, or "natural will," is the tendency of nature towards that which suits it, "a natural force that tends to what conforms to nature, a force that encompasses all the essential properties of nature." Nature in its "natural" state, that is to say, not disfigured by sin, can only wish for the good, since it is "rational," that is to say, tends towards God. The will of a perfect nature is conscious of good, hence adheres to good. But the Fall has clouded this consciousness; nature henceforth tends most often to "anti-nature"; its aspiration gets bogged down in sin. But man is given another will, the θέλησις γνωμική, belonging this time to personhood. It is the will of choice, the personal judgement that I bring to my natural will, either to accept, refuse or direct it towards another goal, to make it truly natural in purging it of sin.

The use of this deliberating will is rendered necessary by the adulteration of our real liberty. "Free-will" corresponds to the state to which sin has reduced us; it is because we are in sin that we must choose without ceasing. That is why, in Christ, there are two "natural" wills, but no human "free-will." The two natural wills cannot enter into conflict in His person, for this person is not a human hypostasis, who, for having tasted the fatal fruit, must ceaselessly choose between good and evil, but a divine hypostasis, one whose choice was made once and for all, that of kenosis, of a non-conditional obedience to the will of the Father.

The human nature of Christ is therefore complete, but what functions as "the person" in man, functions as "the Word" in Christ, whose personhood is divine. Humanity assumed by the latter thus bears a certain likeness to that of Adam before sin. But the kenosis of the Word is also kenosis of this paradisiacal humanity subjected, by the redeeming will of the Saviour, to the objective conditions of sin, conditions to which it must not react by free will, but by suffering and love. On the other hand, if the will of the Son is identical with that of the Father, human will, which becomes that of the Word, is His Own: and in this His own will, resides the entire mystery of our salvation.

IV. Duality and Unity in Christ

The Sixth Ecumenical Council, which met in 681 in Constantinople, clarified the christological definitions of Chalcedon. It reaffirmed the unity and the duality of nature, and specified in Christ the existence of two natural wills which cannot be in opposition, for the human will submits to the divine will as that of God. Quoting a passage from St. Athanasius—an extract from a lost treatise—on the saying of Christ: "Now my soul is troubled . . . Father, save me from this hour" (John 12:27), the Fathers of the Council emphasized that the human will, in the Incarnation, constitutes the very will of the Word. The fact that the Son withholds His own will, and that His will is in consequence no longer that of the Father alone, creates an apparent division between Father and Son. The entire economy of salvation rests in the submission of this, His human will, proper to the Word, to that of God. For human will "enhypostasized" by the Word is not destroyed, just as Christ's flesh, although deified, retains its creaturely reality. "And yet," concluded the Council, "we attribute to the same person the miracles (operated by the energy of the divine) as well as the sufferings (suffered through humanity)."

Behind these definitions lies the anthropology of St. Maximus, which distinguishes between a natural will (θέλησις φυσικὴ) and that deliberating will (θέλησις γνωμικὴ) which is not a tendency of nature, but a possibility of free decision, and hence a dimension of personhood. The θέλησις γνωμική, as choice, gives the moral act its personal character. It does not exist in Christ other than as divine liberty: but one cannot predicate free-will of God, for the single decision of the Son is kenosis, the assumption of the total human condition., total submission to the will of the Father. The proper will of the Word, His human will, submits to the Father, showing by human means—which are not oscillations between "yes" and "no," but "yes" even through the "no" of horror and revolt—the cleaving of the new Adam to his God: "Father, save me from this hour. And yet, it is for this that I have come to this hour; Father, glorify Thy name" (John 12:27-28). "My Father, if it be possible, let this cup pass far from me. Yet, Thy will be done and not mine" (Matt. 26:39). Thus the very attitude of Christ implies freedom, even though St. Maximus denies him free-will. But this freedom is not an everlasting choice that would estrange the Saviour; neither is it the constant necessity for Christ each time to undertake a deliberate choice to submit His deified flesh to the limits of our fallen condition, such as sleep and hunger: for this would make Jesus an actor. Freedom here is regulated by the unique personal consciousness of Christ: it is the definitive and constant choice to assume the unwholesomeness of our condition, even unto the ultimate fatality of death. It is the choice, consented to since eternity, to allow all that makes our condition, that is to say our fallenness, penetrate His self at depth: and this depth is anguish, death, descent into Hell. Contrary to the ascending scheme of the "kenotic" doctrines, if there is a progress in Christ's consciousness, it is in a descent, not a climb. Indeed, for the kenoticists, Christ grows ceaselessly in consciousness of His divinity. Thus it is at baptism that He becomes aware of being the Son of God, by a sort of "reminiscence." But in reading the Gospel we see, to the contrary, the consciousness of the Son descending ever lower, and opening more and more to human degradation. The birth was virginal, an almost paradisiac appearance of deified flesh; the childhood of silent wisdom triumphed without trouble over the wise men; the first miracle at Cana was the miracle of the wedding feast. Then all sinks towards the "hour" for which Christ has come, and for Him the true path of the cross is this conscious grasping whose object is none other than His humanity, this descending exploration of our abyss. It would be absurd to say that the Word became conscious of His divinity, but it is terribly necessary that the Word became conscious of our perdition, and that He takes the sum of it into Himself. For accepting all sin, allowing it to enter Him, Who is without sin, He annuls it. The shadows of the cross reach into a purity they cannot tarnish, and the rending of the cross, into a unity it simply cannot rend.

Christ's agony has often astonished, even scandalized. St. John of Damascus ponders this: "When His human will," he writes, "refused to accept death, and His divine will gave way to this manifestation of humanity, then the Lord, conforming to His human nature, was in torment and fear. He prayed to be spared death. But since His divine will desired His human will to accept death, suffering became voluntary for Christ's humanity." The son of God had to accept death, the result and tribute of sin, by virtue of His human will. But He did not have in Him the root of sin. He could not in consequence know its fruit: death. Man, however, carries in himself this root, and death can be said to be "natural" to him, that is to say, biologically, logically, and psychologically acceptable in the infra-natural state at which God has halted man's fall, and introduced a law which is precisely that of death. Thus the words of the good to the bad thief—"For us it is justice, for we receive what our acts have merited; but He has done nothing blameworthy"—assume an ontological significance. And the good thief dies more easily than Christ. But He, when He accepts the terrible result of sin, when at the bottom of His descent into our meonic gulf He became conscious of death, He sees His deified humanity revolt against this "anti-natural" accursedness. And when the proper will of the Word, that is to say His humanity, submits, He knows a frightful anguish before death, for death is a stranger to Him. Only Christ has known what death really is, since His deified humanity must not die. Only He could take the full measure of agony, since death seized His being from the outside instead of welling up like fate from within, instead of being, as with fallen man, the irreducible kernel of a being mixed with non-being when sickness and time have corrupted his pulp of flesh. And by this measureless death, or rather death measured once, sin is annihilated. It is consumed in the personal unity of Christ on contact with all-powerful divinity: for redemption is nothing other than the gateway to the ultimate separation between man and God through Him Who remained inseparably man and God.

V. Redemption

"It was necessary for us that God become incarnate and die, that we might live again," writes St. Gregory of Nazianzus. And St. Athanasius says: "If God is born and if He dies, it is not because He is born that He dies, but it is to die that He is born." The finality of death was, in effect, not rooted in the human nature of Christ; but His human birth itself had already introduced into His divine person an element which could become mortal. The Incarnation creates as it were a "void" between the Father and Son, an open space that allows for the free submission of the Word made flesh, the spiritual place of redemption. Through dereliction, through accursedness, an innocent person assumes all sin, "substitutes" Himself for those who are justly condemned and suffers death for them. "Behold the Lamb of God Who takes upon Himself the sins of the world," says St. John the Baptist, echoing Isaiah. The entire sacrificial tradition of Israel, beginning with the sacrifice of Isaac replaced by a ram, culminates here. And the whole typology of captivity, every waiting for the liberation of a "remnant," is also fulfilled. St. Paul can write: "Christ has redeemed us from the curse of the Law by becoming a curse for us."

The central moment of the economy of the Son, redemption, must not be separated from the divine plan as a whole. The latter has never changed. Its goal has never ceased being union with God, in all freedom, of personal beings who have themselves fully become hypostases—of the terrestrial cosmos, for men, or the celestial cosmos, for angels. Divine love always pursues the same end: the deification of men, and by them, of the whole universe. But the Fall demands a change, not in God's goal, but in His means, in the divine "pedagogy." Sin has destroyed the primitive plan, that of a direct climb of man to God. A catastrophic fracture has opened in the cosmos; this wound must be healed and the abortive history of man redeemed for a new beginning: such are the aims of redemption.

Redemption, then, appears as the negative facet of the divine plan. It supposes an abnormal reality, tragic, "anti-natural." It would be absurd to fold it about itself, to make it a goal in itself. For the atonement made necessary by our sins is not an end but a means, the means to the only real goal: deification. Salvation itself is only a negative moment: the only essential reality remains union with God. What does it matter being saved from death, from Hell, if it is not to lose oneself in God?

Thus, seen in the light of the divine plan, the redemption assumes several moments, open evermore upon the fullness of the Presence. It is first the abolition of radical obstacles which separate man from God, particularly sin which subjects humanity to the demons and permits the domination of fallen angels upon the terrestrial cosmos. This liberation of the captive creature is later accompanied by a restoration of his nature, rendered capable of receiving grace and going from "glory to glory," even as far as that likeness which takes unto it the nature divine, and allows it to transfigure the cosmos.

The immensity of this work of Christ, a work incomprehensible to the angels, so St. Paul tells us, cannot then be enclosed in a single explanation nor in a single metaphor. The very idea of redemption assumes a plainly legal aspect: it is the atonement of the slave, the debt paid for those who remained in prison because they could not discharge it. Legal also is the theme of the mediator who reunited man to God through the cross. But these two Pauline images, stressed again by the Fathers, must not be allowed to harden, for this would be to build an indefensible relationship of rights between God and humanity. Rather must we relocate them among the almost infinite number of other images, each like a facet of an event ineffable in itself. Looming large in the Gospel are the Good Shepherd seeking the lost sheep, "the strong man" who triumphs over the brigand, ties him up and takes his spoils from him, the woman who rediscovers and cleans the drachma where the image of God lies printed beneath the dust of sin. Liturgical texts, particularly during Holy Week, have for their *leit-motif* the theme of the victorious warrior who destroys the enemies, and breaks down the gates of Hell where, as Dante writes, "their banners enter in triumph." There abound also in the Fathers images of a physical order: that of the purifying fire, and particularly that of the doctor who heals the wounds of his people. Indeed, since Origen, Christ is the Good Samaritan who tends and restores human nature wounded by brigands, that is, by the demons. Finally, the theme of sacrifice is much more than a metaphor. It is the culmination of a typology which participates in the very reality it announces, in the "blood of Christ" offered "in a spirit of eternity," as is written in the Epistle to the Hebrews, where this image completes in depth the legal symbolism.

Freely taking our place, Christ "is become a curse," writes St. Paul to the Galatians. The dereliction of Christ on the cross is therefore necessary, for God departs from the accursed, from the alien forsaken by all. "My God, my God, why hast Thou forsaken me?" This total nakedness of anguish also has a symbolic value: for the ultimate cry of the Crucified is none other than the first verse of Psalm 21, the prayer of the long-suffering man of righteousness. The beginning of this psalm proclaims human despair: "I am as running water, and all my bones are out of joint." Then follows the famous prophetic passage, the hands and feet pierced, the garments shared out, the tunic tossed for. Thus, by an inner typology, Christ's passion corresponds, and responds, to the estrangement, to the agony of human nature devastated by its fallenness. And the end of the psalm, like one announcing the Resurrection, sings the triumph of righteousness and the saving power of God.

If Christ reiterates this psalm, it is because he assumes our total condition, even to the limits of that feeling, known to the dying when they die religiously—when, that is, they know death as that passing where nature, limited, exteriorized, fallen since birth, is shattered—that feeling of being abandoned by God: "depart not from me, for anguish holds me: approach Thou me, for no one aids me." And yet, there is neither rending nor tragedy in the Word, eternally consubstantial with the Father. And that is why, penetrating into Christ, rending and tragedy are ended. "When Christ remained voluntarily prisoner, death suffered the pangs of childbirth," says St. John Chrysostom in an Easter sermon. "It could not resist, it bursts forth, it frees us." And Maximus the Confessor continues the redemptive theme with the words: "Christ's death on the cross has been the judgement of judgement." Unable to function in the person of the Son of God, malediction becomes benediction; by the cross, all the conditions of sin become conditions of salvation. Henceforth neither sin nor death separates us any longer from God. For baptism enshrouds us in the death of Christ to raise us up with Him; for penitence can always take us back to God, and death, daily assumed by penitence, can open for us the life divine.

The curse of death has never been a judgement of God. It was the punishment of a loving Father, not the obtuse anger of a tyrant. Its character was educative and restorative. It prevented the perpetuation of an estranged life, the apathetic induction into an anti-natural condition. It not only put a limit to the decomposition of our nature, but, by the anguish of finitude, helped man to become alive to his condition and turn to God. Similarly, the unjust will of Satan cannot function except through the just permission of God. Satan's choice was not only limited by the divine will, but also used by it, as we see in the case of Job.

Thus neither death nor Satan's domination have ever been purely negative. They were already the signs and means of divine love. But at the moment of redemption, the demonic powers are dispossessed, and a change occurs in the relations of man and God. God, we might say, modifies his pedagogy. He takes from Satan the right to dominate humanity. Sin is banished, and the dominion of the Evil One crumbles. The word atonement thus acquires here another sense: that of a debt repaid to the devil, as patristic literature of the early centuries emphasized. God gave a power to the devil, then took it from him, for transgressing his rights in assailing an innocent. Irenaeus, Origen, and Gregory of Nyssa all show how Satan, wishing to take into his power the only being over whom he had none, is justly dispossessed. Certain Fathers, especially Gregory of Nyssa, propose the symbol of a divine ruse: on the hook of His divinity, the humanity of Christ is the bait; the devil throws himself on the prey, but the hook pierces him—he cannot swallow God, and dies.

A debt paid to God, a debt to the devil: two images which have value only together, to encompass the act in its incomprehensible depth through which Christ returned to us the dignity of sons of God. A theology impoverished by that rationalism which recoils before these, the images of the Fathers, necessarily loses the cosmological perspective of Christ's work. But rather than this, we must enlarge our sense of redemption. For it is not only the demons but also the angels who are dispossessed, relatively speaking. In the second Adam, God Himself unites directly with humanity, causing it to participate in His boundless superiority over the angels. Redemption is a wondrous reality, which extends across the entire cosmos, visible or not. "The judgement of judgement" reconciles the fallen cosmos with God. God on the cross extends His arms to humanity. As St. Gregory of Nazianzus writes, "A few drops of blood make the universe whole again."

The devil has been crushed, but without his rights being wronged, so to speak. The law of mortal nature has been revoked, but again without anything of divine justice being wronged. In other words, we should not depict God either as a constitutional monarch subject to a justice that goes beyond him, or as a tyrant whose whim would create a law without order or objectivity. Justice is not an abstract reality superior to God but an expression of His nature. Just as He freely creates yet manifests Himself in the order and beauty of creation, so He manifests Himself in His justice: Christ Who is Himself justice, affirms in His fullness God's justice. It is not that the Son effects an outlandish justice by bearing an infinite satisfaction for a vengeance not less infinite than the Father. "Why," asks Gregory of Nazianzus, "why should the blood of the Son be pleasing to the Father Who did not even want to accept Isaac offered up in a burnt-offering by Abraham, but replaced this human sacrifice by that of a ram?"

Christ does not execute justice; He manifests it: He manifests that which God expects from the creature, the fullness of humanity, "the maximum man" to take up the expression of Nicholas of Cusa. He fulfills the vocation of man betrayed by Adam: to live, and to nourish the universe, only from God. Such is God's justice. The Son, identical with God in His divine nature, acquires through the Incarnation the possibility of fulfilling it. For He can then submit to the Father as if He were distant from Him, renounce this will of His own given Him by His humanity, and give Himself totally, even unto death, that the Father may be glorified. God's justice is that man should be no longer separated from God. It is the restoration of humanity in Christ, the true Adam. "Is it not obvious that the Father accepts the sacrifice, not because He demanded it or felt some need for it, but by economy," concludes St. Gregory of Nazianzus. "Man had to be sanctified by God's humanity; He Himself had to free us, triumphing over the tyrant by His Own strength, had to recall us to Him by His Son Who is the Mediator, fulfilling all for the honor of the Father, to Whom He is obedient in everything . . . Let the rest be venerated by silence."

VI. Resurrection

The Father accepts the Son's sacrifice "by economy": "man had to be sanctified by God's humanity" (St. Gregory of Nazianzus, Oration 45, *On the Holy Pascha*). Kenosis culminates and ends with Christ's death, to sanctify the entire human condition, including death. *Cur Deus homo?* Not only because of our sins but for our sanctification, to introduce all the moments of our fallen life into that true life which never knows death. By Christ's resurrection, the fullness of life is inserted into the dry tree of humanity.

Christ's work therefore presents a physical, even biological, reality. On the cross, death is swallowed up in life. In Christ, death enters into divinity and there exhausts itself, for "it does not find a place there." Redemption thus signifies a struggle of life against death, and the triumph of life. Christ's humanity constitutes the first fruits of a new creation. Through it a force for life is introduced into the cosmos to resurrect and transfigure it in the final destruction of death. Since the Incarnation and the Resurrection death is enervated, is no longer absolute. Everything converges towards the ἀποκατάστασις τῶν πάντων, that is to say, towards the complete restoration of all that is destroyed by death, towards the embracing of the whole cosmos by the glory of God become all in all things, without excluding from this fullness the freedom of each person before that full consciousness of his wretchedness which the light divine will communicate to him.

And so we must complete the legal image of redemption by a sacrificial image. Redemption is also the sacrifice where Christ, following the Epistle to the Hebrews, appears as the eternal sacrificer, the High Priest according to the order of Melchizedek Who finishes in heaven what He began on earth. Death on the cross is the Passover of the New Alliance, fulfilling in one reality all that is symbolized by the Hebrew Passover. For freedom from death and the introduction of human nature into God's Kingdom realize the only true Exodus. This sacrifice, this surrender of will itself to which Adam could not consent, certainly represents an expiation. But above all, it represents a sacrament, sacrament *par excellence*, the free gift to God, by Christ in His humanity, of the first fruits of creation, the fulfillment of that immense sacramental action, devolving first upon Adam, which the new humanity must complete, the offering of the cosmos as receptacle of grace. The Resurrection operates a change in fallen nature, opens a prodigious possibility: the possibility of sanctifying death itself. Henceforth, death is no longer an impasse, but a door to the Kingdom. Grace is given back to us, and if we carry it as "clay vessels," or receptacles still mortal, our fragility will now take on a power which vanquishes death. The peaceful assurance of martyrs, insensible not only to fear but to physical pain itself, proves that an effective awareness of the Resurrection is henceforth possible to the Christian.

St. Gregory of Nyssa has well emphasized this sacramental character of the Passion. Christ, he said, did not wait to be forced by Judas's betrayal, the wickedness of the priests, or the people's lack of awareness: "He anticipated this will of evil, and before being forced, gave Himself freely on the eve of the Passion, Holy Thursday, by giving His flesh and blood." It is the sacrifice of the immolated lamb before the beginning of the world that is so freely fulfilled here. The true Passion begins on Holy Thursday, but in total freedom.

Soon after came Gethsemane, then the cross. Death on the cross is that of a divine person: submitted to by the humanness of Christ, it is consciously suffered by His eternal hypostasis. And the separation of body and soul, the fundamental aspect of death, also breaks in upon the God-man. The soul that descends to Hell remains "enhypostasized" in the Word, and also the body hanging on the cross. Similarly, the human person remains equally present in His body recaptured by the elements, as in His soul. That is why we venerate the relics of the saints. But even more so is this true in the case of Christ, for divinity remains attached both to the body which slumbers the "pure sleep" of Holy Saturday in the sepulchre, and to the victorious soul which batters down the doors of Hell. How, indeed, could death destroy this person who suffers it in all its tragic estrangement, since this person is divine? That is why the Resurrection is already present in the death of Christ. Life springs from the tomb; it is manifested by death, in the very death of Christ. Human nature triumphs over an anti-natural condition. For it is, in its entirety, gathered up in Christ, "recapitulated" by Him, to adopt the expression of St. Irenaeus. Christ is the Head of the Church, that is to say, of the new humanity in whose heart no sin, no adverse power can henceforth finally separate man from grace. In Christ, a man's life can always begin afresh, however burdened with sin. A man can always surrender his life to Christ, so that He may restore it to him, liberated and whole. And this work of Christ is valid for the entire assemblage of humanity, even beyond the visible limits of the Church. All faith in the triumph of life over death, every presentiment of the Resurrection, are implicit belief in Christ: for only the power of Christ raises, and will raise, the dead. Since the victory of Christ over death, the Resurrection has become universal law for creation; and not only for humanity, but for the beasts, the plants and the stones, for the whole cosmos in which each one of us is the head. We are baptized in the death of Christ, shrouded in water to rise again with Him. And for the soul lustrated in the baptismal waters of tears, and ablaze with the fire of the Holy Spirit, the Resurrection is not only hope but present reality. The parousia begins in the souls of the saints, and St. Simeon the New Theologian can write: "For those who became children of the light and sons of the day to come, for those who always walk in the light, the Day of the Lord will never come, for they are already with God and in God." An infinite ocean of light flows from the risen body of the Lord.

Postscript

IMAGE AND LIKENESS

Although man contains in himself all the elements which form the world, his true perfection, of which he could rightly be proud, lies not in this. "There is nothing remarkable," says St. Gregory of Nyssa, "to want to make of man the image and likeness of the universe; for the earth passes away, the sky changes and all that is contained therein is as transient as the container." "It has been said that man is a microcosm. Thinking to exalt human nature by this imposing name, men did not notice that it invested man with the qualities of both mosquitoes and mice."[1] Man's perfection lies not in that which likens him to the rest of creation, but in that which distinguishes him from the cosmos and likens him to his Creator. Divine revelation teaches that man was made in the image and likeness of God.

All the Fathers of both the Eastern and Western Churches saw in the very fact that man was created in God's image and likeness a certain primordial congruence between man's being and God's being. However, the theological expressions of this revealed truth were often different, though not altogether contradictory, in the Eastern and Western traditions. St. Augustine, striving to form an idea of God, starts with the image of God in us and tries to rediscover in God what is found in our soul, created in His image. This method of psychological analogies is applied to the knowledge of God, to theology. St. Gregory of Nyssa, on the other hand, selects as a point of departure what the revelation tells us of God in order to find in man what corresponds to the image of God. This theological method

[1]*On the Structure of Man*, XVI, P.G. 44, col. 177D-180A.

is applied to the science of man, to anthropology. The first way tries to know God by starting from man created in His image. The second way wants to define man's true nature by starting from the concept of God, in Whose image man was made.

If we wish to find in the Holy Fathers' works a clear definition of what corresponds in us to God's image, we risk getting lost amidst different assertions which, while not being contradictory, cannot be applied to any part of man's being. Indeed, either the lineaments of God's image are attributed to man's sovereign character, his domination over the physical cosmos, or God's image is sought in the spiritual nature of man, in the soul, or in the principal part, ruling (ἡγεμονικὸν) his being, in the mind (νοῦς), in the higher faculties, such as the intellect, the reason (λόγος), or in the free capacity proper to man of inner self-determination (αὐτεξουσία) by whose virtue man himself becomes the initiator of his actions. Sometimes God's image is likened to some quality of the soul, its simplicity or its immortality, or it is identified with the soul's capacity to know God, to live in communion with Him in the presence of the Holy Spirit in man's soul. Sometimes, as in the *Spiritual Homilies* attributed to St. Macarius of Egypt, the image of God presents itself in two ways. It is, first of all, the formal freedom of man, freedom of the will or freedom of choice, which cannot be destroyed by sin; secondly, it is the "heavenly image," that is, the positive content of God's image. Such was the communion with God that invested man's being, before the Fall, with the Word and the Holy Spirit.[2] Finally, as in St. Irenaeus of Lyon, St. Gregory of Nyssa and St. Gregory Palamas, not only the soul, but also man's body shares the image of God, having been created in His image. "The name 'man,'" says St. Gregory Palamas, "is not applied separately to the soul or to the body, but to both together, for together they were made in the image of God."[3]

[2]*Spiritual Homilies*, XII, 1, 6, 7, and so on. P.G. 34, col. 557-561, Russian translation (Sergiev Posad, 1904) 93 and ff.

[3]*Prosopopeia*, P.G. 150, col. 1361C. This work is attributed to St. Gregory Palamas.

Man, according to St. Gregory Palamas, was made in God's image to a greater degree than were the angels, because His spirit, joined to man's body, possessed an animating power with which He energizes and controls man's body. It is this capacity that the angels, as bodiless spirits, lack, although they are even closer to God through the simplicity of their spiritual nature.[4]

These multiple and diverse definitions show that the thinking of the Holy Fathers seeks to avoid limiting to any single part of man's being what relates to the divine image. Indeed, the biblical narrative does not specify the characteristic lineaments of God's image, but presents the very creation of man as a special act, different from the creation of other beings. Like the angels, who were created, as St. Isaac the Syrian expresses it, "in silence,"[5] man was not formed by the divine command given to the earth. Instead, God Himself formed him from the dust of the earth with His own hands, that is, as St. Irenaeus of Lyon understands it, with the Word and the Spirit,[6] and He breathed into him the breath of life. St. Gregory of Nazianzus interprets this passage in Genesis in the following way: "The Word, having taken a clod of the newly-made earth, with immortal hands formed my image and imparted to it His life, because He sent into it His Spirit, which is the effluence of the unknown divinity. Thus out of dust and breath was man made in the image of the immortal one, because in them both the nature of spirit is supreme. Accordingly, in my quality of earth, I am attached to life here below, but being also a divine particle, I bear in my breast the desire for a future life."[7] In this same poem dedicated to the soul, he says: "The soul is a breath of God, and, though

[4]The physical, theological chapters and so on (38 and 39). Ibid., col. 1145-1148.

[5]Ed. A. J. Wensinck (Amsterdam, 1923) p. 127.

[6]*Against Heresies*, IV, preface, § 4, P.G. 7, col. 975, and also IV, 20, 1 (1032); V, 1, 3 (1123); V, 5, 1 (1134-5); V, 6, 1 (1136-7); V, 28, 3 (1200).

[7]*Poëmata Dogmatica*, VIII, Περὶ ψυχῆς vv. 70-75. P.G. 37, col. 452; Russian translation, Seventh Oration, "On the Soul." *Works*, part IV, pp. 199-200.

heavenly, it suffers a mingling with the earthly. It is the light enclosed in a cave, although it is divine and inextinguishable."[8]

To take these words literally, we must apparently infer from these two extracts the uncreated character of the soul and see in man a god burdened with a bodily nature, or at least the mingling of god and animal. Understood in this way, creation of man in God's image would contradict the Christian teaching which sees in man a creature, destined to attain union with God, to become god by grace, but certainly not God by his very origin. Even without mentioning other improbable consequences of such a supposition, the problem of evil would be incomprehensible because of it: either Adam could not sin, since, being God in his soul, he was a particle of divinity, or else original sin would also be reflected upon divine nature, so that God Himself would have sinned in Adam. St. Gregory of Nazianzus totally refuted such a point of view. In his oration on man's nature, he addresses his soul thus: "And if you are truly God's breath and of God's design, as you think yourself, O my soul, then put aside all untruth that I may believe in you . . . How can you so trouble yourself with the insinuations of the destructive Adversary if you are united with the heavenly Spirit? If even with such aid you bow down to the earth, then, alas, alas, how all-powerful must be your destructive sin."[9] The soul, mingled (κιρναμένη) with the "heavenly Spirit," is aided, consequently, by something higher than itself. Only the presence in it of divine energy allows it to be called a "particle of divinity" for it takes its source from the divine effluence breathed into it, which is grace. "The divine breath indicates the method of man's creation by virtue of which man's spirit, closely bound to grace, is produced, just as a movement of air is produced by the breath, containing this breath and inseparable from it." This is the communion with divine energy, inherent in the soul, which is denoted by

[8]Ibid., vv. 1-3, col. 446-447; Russian translation, part IV, p. 197.

[9]*Poëmata Moralia,* XIV. Περὶ τῆς ἀνθρωπίνης φύσεως, vv. 76-84. Ibid., col. 761-762. Russian translation, Tenth Oration, "On Human Nature." *Works,* part IV, pp. 214-215.

the term "particle of divinity." Indeed, in one of his *Homilies*, St. Gregory of Nazianzus speaks of communion with the divine being, referring to the "three lights," of which the first is God, "the highest, ineffable Light; the second, the angels, a certain effluence (ἀπορροή τις) of or communion (μετουσία) with the first Light; the third light, man, also called light, because his spirit is lit by the primordial Light, which is God."[10] Thus creation in God's image and likeness implies communion with the divine being, with God. This means that communion presupposes grace.

The image of God in man, as far as it is authentic, is, according to St. Gregory of Nyssa, necessarily unknowable, for, reflecting the plenitude of its prototype, it too must possess the unknowability of the divine being. That is also why it is impossible to define what constitutes God's image in man. We cannot conceive it otherwise than through the idea of communion with the infinite goodness of God: "God by His nature is goodness itself," says St. Gregory of Nyssa. "Or rather, God transcends in goodness everything that man can conceive or comprehend. Consequently, He made human life from no other impulse than because He is good. Being such and having undertaken for this reason alone the creation of human nature, He did not wish to manifest only half the powers of His goodness, endowing with a part of His goodness, while jealously refusing to share the remainder. The very perfection of goodness is manifested in Him by the fact that He calls man forth from non-being to being and abundantly imparts to him everything that is good. The number of these blessings is so great that it is impossible to enumerate them. They are, however, contained briefly in the saying that man was made in God's image. For this is like saying that God made human nature a communicant of everything good. . . . But if the image was identical with the beatitude of the prototype, man would not merely be His image, but would merge with Him. What distinction would we notice between the divine being and what resembles Him? The following: namely, that the divine being was uncreated,

[10]Fortieth Oration, "On Holy Baptism," 5, P.G. 36, col. 364BC. Russian translation *Works*, part III, p. 226.

while man exists by virtue of a creative act."[11] It is obvious that St. Gregory of Nyssa understands here by the image of God the ultimate perfection, the state of man's deification, participating in the plenitude (πλήρωμα) of the divine being, in the abundance of divine goodness. That is why, speaking of God's image in man, limited in that man shares only certain blessings, of an image as yet incomplete, he sees lineaments characteristic to man as being made in God's image, in particular "in that man is liberated from necessity and is not subject to the sovereignty of nature, but can determine himself according to his own judgement. For virtue is independent and is her own mistress."[12] This is, so to say, the "formal" image, the necessary condition in order for man to attain perfect likeness to God. As far as man is made in the image of God, he is presented as a personal being who is not to be ruled by nature, but who can himself rule nature, likening it to his divine prototype.

Man's person is not a part of man's being, just as the persons of the Holy Trinity are not parts of God. That is why the character of God's image does not refer to one element of man's composition, but refers to all of human nature. The first man, containing in himself all of human nature, was also the unique person: "For the name Adam," says St. Gregory of Nyssa, "is not now given to a created object, as in subsequent narratives. For created man has no special name; he is universal man, encompassing in himself all of humanity. So then, by this designation of Adam's universal nature, we are led to understand that divine providence and energy embrace in primordial creation the whole human race. For God's image is not confined to one part of nature, nor grace to only one individual among those belonging to it, but their activity extends over the whole human race. . . . There is no distinction between the man formed at the beginning of the world's creation, and him who will come at its end: they bear in themselves the same image of God. Consequently, man made in God's image is nature

[11]*On the Structure of Man*, XVI, P.G. 44, 184AC.

[12]*On the Structure of Man*, col. 184B.

understood as a whole, reflecting the likeness of God."[13] God's image, proper to Adam's person, relates to all of humanity, to "universal man." That is why in Adam's race the multiplicity of persons, each of whom bears God's image (one may say this is the multiplying of God's image in the plurality of human hypostases), in no way contradicts the ontological unity of the nature common to all men. Quite the opposite: a human person cannot realize the fullness to which he is called, the fullness of becoming the perfect image of God, if he appropriates a part of the nature, considering it to be his personal property. For God's image in man attains its perfection only when human nature becomes like God's nature, when it begins fully to participate in uncreated goodness. Only one nature exists, common to all men, although it appears to us fragmented by sin, parcelled out among many persons. This original unity of nature, re-established in the Church, appeared to the Apostle Paul so complete that he referred to it as the Body of Christ.

So then, men possess a single common nature in many human persons. This distinction of nature and person in man is no less difficult to understand than the analogical difference between a single nature and three persons in God. One must first of all take into account that the person is unknown to us, that is, the human hypostasis in its true expression, free from every admixture. What we usually call "persons" or "personal" denotes rather individuals or individual. We have grown accustomed to see in these two terms—person and individual—virtual synonyms. We use them both indiscriminately to denote one and the same thing. However, in the accepted sense, "individual" and "person" have opposite meanings, for "individual" expresses some mixture of the person with elements belonging to common nature, while "person" denotes what is distinguished from nature. In our present condition we know a person through the individual and as the individual. When we want to define, to characterize a person, we gather up the individual characteristics, the character traits, which are also found,

[13]Ibid., col. 185-204.

however, in other individuals. Since they belong to common nature, these traits are never completely "personal." Ultimately, we conclude that what is for us most dear in some human being, what precisely makes him "himself," remains undefinable, for in his nature there is nothing that would belong properly to his own person, always unique, incomparable, having none other like itself. The man ruled by his nature and acting according to his natural properties, according to his character, is the least personal. He establishes himself as an individual, as the possessor of his own nature, his "I" which he sets in opposition to the natures of other individuals, thus confusing person and nature. This confusion proper to fallen humanity, in the ascetic literature of the Eastern Church, is called *samost'* (αὐτότης, φιλαυτία), whose true meaning cannot be conveyed by the word "egoism."

We experience some difficulty in connection with the christological dogma, which considers will as a function of nature. It is easier for us to imagine the person as something which determines itself and forces us to recognize it by virtue of its will. However, the idea of the person implies the idea of freedom in relation to nature. The person is free from, and undetermined by, its nature. The human hypostasis can only reveal itself by renouncing its own will, because the latter determines us and subjects us to natural necessity. Everything individual, everything self-determining, in which the person is confused with nature and thereby loses its true freedom, must be destroyed. This is the basic principle of asceticism: the voluntary renunciation of personal will, of the chimera of individual freedom in order to rediscover true freedom, the freedom of the person, which is also the image of God proper to every man. That is why, according to St. Nilus of Sinai, the perfect monk "regards, after God, every man as God Himself."[14] Another man's person will appear as God's image to him who knows how to renounce his individual limitations in

[14] *On Prayer*, ch. 123, P.G. 79, col. 1193C; Russian translation, *Love of Goodness*, V. 2 (3rd ed. Moscow, 1913) p. 222 (ch. 121).

order to rediscover the common nature, and in this very way to attain the flowering of his own person.

What corresponds in us to God's image is not a part of our nature, but the person including nature in itself. Leontius of Byzantium, a theologian of the sixth century, for the nature confined in any person uses the special term "ἐνυπόστατον," "enhypostasized," that is, such as is found in a hypostasis or person. All nature, he declares, is enclosed in a hypostasis, such being the nature of a hypostasis that cannot exist otherwise.[15] But on the lower stages of being, hypostases denote individuals, individual beings. They denote persons only when it is a matter of spiritual beings such as men, angels or God. In the case of the person (and not the individual), a hypostasis does not divide the nature, generating several separate natures. The Holy Trinity is not three gods, but only one. If the multiplicity of human persons fragments nature, parcels it out to a multitude of individuals, that is because we know of no other generation than that which appeared after the Fall, when human nature lost its likeness to divine nature. We have seen that for St. Gregory of Nyssa and St. Maximus the Confessor, the very creation of Eve already becomes an act wrought by God in the foreknowledge of sin and its consequences for humanity. However Eve, taken from Adam, "bone of his bone and flesh of his flesh," a new human person, completed Adam's nature, was of the same nature, "the same flesh." Only in consequence of sin did these two first human persons become two separate natures, two individual beings, having between themselves external relationships—"and your desire will be for your husband, and he will be lord over you" (Genesis 3:16). After the Fall of the first people, human nature became divided, fragmented, parcelled out to a multiplicity of individuals. Man shows himself in a double aspect: as individual nature, he becomes a part of the whole, one of the component elements of the world; but as person, he is by no means a part, he contains everything in himself. The nature is the content

[15]*Against Nestorius and Eutyches*. P.G. 86, col. 1277CD. These same ideas are developed by St. Maximus the Confessor (P.G. 91, col. 557-560) and St. John of Damascus, *An Accurate Account of the Orthodox Faith*, 1, IX, 53.

of the person; the person is the image of this nature's existence. A person, affirming himself as an individual and confining himself to the limits of his separate nature, cannot flower fully and grows impoverished. Only by renouncing his own content, freely giving it up, ceasing to exist for himself alone, does a person fully express himself in the single nature of all. Renouncing his separate good, he endlessly expands, and is enriched by everything that belongs to all. A person becomes the perfect image of God by discovering His likeness, which is the perfection of the nature common to all men. The distinction between persons and nature reproduces in humanity the order of divine life, expressed by the dogma of the Trinity. This is the basis of all Christian anthropology, of all evangelical morality, for, according to St. Gregory of Nyssa, "Christianity is the imitation of God's nature."[16]

Made in the image of God, man is a personal being, confronting a personal God. God addresses him as a person, and man responds to God. St. Basil the Great said that man is a creature who received the command to become god.[17] But this command addressed to human freedom is not coercion. As a personal being, man can accept or reject God's will. He will remain a person, however far he may stray from God and lose His likeness in his nature. This means that God's image in man is indestructible. Man will remain a personal being by fulfilling God's will, by showing a perfect likeness to Him in his nature. For, according to St. Gregory of Nazianzus, "to respect man's freedom, God placed in Paradise this man so that goodness might belong equally to the man who chose it and to him who laid in its first seeds."[18] Consequently, whether man chooses good or evil, whether he manifests God's likeness or "unlikeness," he

[16]*De Professione Christiana.* P.G. 46, col. 244C.

[17]The words of St. Basil the Great reported by St. Gregory of Nazianzus in the Forty-third Oration, "Funeral Oration to Basil, archbishop of the Cappadocian Caesarea," 48, P.G. 36, col. 560A. Russian translation of the *Works* of St. Gregory of Nazianzus, part IV.

[18]Forty-fifth Oration, "On Holy Easter," 8, P.G. 36, col. 632C. Russian translation, part IV (Moscow, 1889) p. 129.

freely possesses his nature, because he is a person made in the image of God. However, as far as the person is inseparable from the nature existing in it, so far every flaw, every "unlikeness" of the nature limits the person, obscures in it "the image of God." In fact, if we possess freedom, insofar as we are persons, then the will with which we act is a property of our nature. In the words of St. Maximus the Confessor, the will is a "natural force directed to what is consistent with nature, a force which embraces all the essential properties of nature."[19] St. Maximus distinguishes this natural will (θέλημα φυσικόν), which is the desire for good sought by rational nature, from the will which chooses (θέλημα γνωμικὸν) and belongs to the person.[20] The nature wills and acts, but the person chooses; it accepts or rejects what nature wills. However, according to St. Maximus, this freedom of choice is already a flaw, a limitation of true freedom: perfect nature has no need of choice, for it knows what is good in a natural way. Its freedom is based on this knowledge. Our freedom of will (γνώμη) reveals the imperfection of fallen human nature, the loss of God's likeness. Since this nature is obscured by sin, it does not know its true good and is directed constantly to what is "anti-nature." Thus the human person is always confronted by the necessity of choice. It gropes its way forward. This vacillation in the ascent to what is good is known as "freedom of will." The person, called to union with God, to perfect assimilation through grace of his nature with divine nature, is bound to a mutilated nature, crippled by sin, ravaged by contradictory desires. Knowing and willing according to this imperfect nature, the person is, in practice, blind and weak. It no longer knows how to choose, and too often yields to the impulses of a nature which has become the slave of sin. In this way, what was made in us in God's image is drawn down into the abyss, although it still retains its freedom of choice and its ability to return to God.

[19] *Opuscula Theologica et Polemica, Ad Marinum,* P.G. 91, col. 45D-48A.

[20] Ibid., col. 48A-49A, col. 192BC. Compare with St. John of Damascus, *An Accurate Account of the Orthodox Faith,* III, 14, P.G. 94, col. 1036-1037, 1044-1045.

Man was made perfect. Yet this does not mean that his original state coincided with the ultimate aim, that he was in union with God from the moment of creation. Until the Fall, Adam was neither "pure nature" nor deified man. As already mentioned, the cosmology and the anthropology of the Eastern Church have a dynamic character, and exclude every external combination of the ideas of nature and grace. They interpenetrate each other, exist in one another. St. John of Damascus sees the profoundest mystery in the fact that man was created "by virtue of his own desire for God, transformed into god through communion with divine illumination."[21] The perfection of our first nature was primarily expressed in this capacity to unite with God, to cling ever more to the plenitude of the divine being, a plenitude which was to penetrate and transfigure created nature. St. Gregory of Nazianzus referred precisely to this higher faculty of the human spirit when he spoke of God breathing into man with His breath a "particle of His divinity," that is grace. Grace is present from the beginning in the soul, and the latter is capable of receiving and assimilating this deifying energy. For the human person was called, in the words of St. Maximus the Confessor, "to bring together in love created nature and uncreated nature, showing them in unity and identity by the acquisition of grace."[22] Unity and identity relate here to the person, to the human hypostasis. So then, man was to bring together in grace two natures in his created hypostasis, to become a "created god," a "god by grace," in contrast to Christ, Who, although a divine person, assumed human nature. The reciprocal action of both wills is necessary to attain this end: on the one hand, deifying divine will, endowing grace through the Holy Spirit Who is present in the human person; on the other hand, the human will, which submits to the divine will in that it accepts grace, assimilates it and allows it to penetrate all its nature. Thus, as the will is an active force in rational nature, it acts through grace to the same degree that nature par-

[21]*An Accurate Account of the Orthodox Faith*, II, P.G. 94, col. 924A. Russian translation, p. 213.

[22]*De ambiguis*. P.G. 91, col. 1308A.

ticipates in grace and becomes anew the likeness of God by means of the "transforming fire."[23]

The Fathers of the Greek Church presented human nature thus: either as the tripartite composition of spirit, soul and body (νοῦς, ψυχή, σῶμα), or as the union of soul and body. The distinction between the advocates of trichotomism and dichotomism reduces generally to one of terminology. The dichotomists see in the νοῦς the higher faculty of the rational soul, the faculty by whose virtue man enters into communion with God. The person or the human hypostasis contains all the parts of this natural composition, expresses itself in all men who exist in it and through it. Made in God's image, it is the constant origin of human nature, dynamic and changeable, directed always by its will to an external end. It may be said that the image is a divine seal, stamped on the nature and placing it in a personal relation with God, a perfectly unique relationship for every human being. This relationship is made real by means of the will which directs the whole nature to God, in Whom man must find all the fullness of his being: "For the human soul," says St. Tikhon Zadonsky, "is a spirit made by God, and only in God, by Whom it was made in His image and likeness, can it discover contentment, repose, peace, solace and joy; and when it strays from Him, it is forced to find its pleasures in created things and different passions, and must feed itself on husks; but it does not find proper repose and joy and dies from hunger. For spiritual food is needful to the human spirit."[24] The human spirit must find nurture in God, live in God; the soul must nourish the spirit; the body must live in the soul—such was the original design of man's immortal nature. Turning away from God, however, the spirit, instead of giving food to the soul, begins to live at the soul's expense, feeding itself with its substance (this is what are usually called "spiritual values"). The soul, in its turn, be-

[23]The expression "πῦρ τῆς ἀλλαγῆς" belongs to Diadochus of Photice, "The Oration on the Ascetic," ch. XVII, ed. K. Popov (Kiev, 1903) vol. 1, p. 363.

[24]"How God Calls the Sinner to Repentance," § 140, *Works* of St. Tikhon Zadonsky (6th ed. Moscow, 1898) vol. 1, p. 215.

gins to live from the life of the body, and this is the origin of the passions. Finally, the body, compelled to seek its food in the external world, in soulless matter, in the end discovers death. Man's structure falls to pieces.

Evil entered into the world through the will of man. It is not a nature (φύσις), but a condition (ἕξις). "The nature of good is stronger than the habit of evil," says Diadochus of Photice, "for good exists while evil does not, or rather, it exists only at that moment when it is put into practice."[25] According to St. Gregory of Nyssa, sin is a sickness of the will, which errs in taking for good the mere illusion of good. That is why even the very desire to taste the fruit of the knowledge of good and evil was already a sin, for, according to St. Gregory, knowledge presupposes a certain disposition towards the object that one desires to know. Consequently, evil, not existing by itself, ought not to have been known.[26] Evil becomes real only by means of the will, which is the sole reason for its existence. It is precisely the will that gives evil a certain being. That man, naturally disposed to know and love God, should have striven with his will after non-existent good, after an illusory end, could only be explained as the effect of an external influence, the insinuation of an alien will to which the human will gave its assent.[27] Before entering into the earthly world through Adam's will, evil had found its origin in the spiritual world. It was the will of angels eternally resolved to be hostile towards God that first gave birth to evil. Evil is the attraction of the will towards non-being, the negation of creation, and of God, and it is, particularly, a violent hatred of grace, to which the rebellious will is obdurately opposed. Although they have become spirits of darkness, the fallen angels still remain creatures of God's making, but in their self-determination, which is opposed to God's will, they are

[25]"The Oration on the Ascetic," ch. III, ed. Popov (Kiev, 1903) vol. 1, pp. 24-25. The Latin translation, entitled *Capita de perfectione spirituali*, P.G. 65, col. 1168.

[26]*On the Structure of Man*, XX, P.G. 44, col. 197-200. "On the Lord's Prayer," IV, ibid., col. 1161D-1164A.

[27]Ibid., col. 200C.

possessed by a desperate striving for a non-being that they will never attain. Their eternal descent into the abyss will have no end. St. Seraphim of Sarov said of the demons: "They are abominable; their conscious resistance to grace turned them into angels of darkness, into unimaginable monsters. But being by nature angels, they possess immense power. The least of them could destroy the earth, if divine grace had not rendered powerless their hatred of God's creation. But they strive to destroy creation from within, by directing human freedom to evil."[28] Referring to an ascetic translation attributed to St. Anthony,[29] St. Seraphim distinguishes three wills acting in man. The first is the will of God, the perfect and redemptive will; the second is the will of man, which, while not necessarily destructive, is not in itself a redemptive will; finally, there is the demonic will, which seeks our destruction.

In Orthodox asceticism, there are special terms to denote the diverse effects exerted by the evil spirits on man's soul. There are the "thoughts" (λογισμοὶ) or images, rising up out of the lower regions of the soul, from the subconscious.[30] Then there is the "seduction" (προσβολή), that is the presence of an alien thought, arriving from without and introduced by a hostile will into the consciousness. "It is not a sin," says St. Mark the Hermit, "but a witness to our freedom."[31] Sin begins only with the "union" (συγκατάθεσις),[32] that is the cleaving of the mind to the intruded thought or image. Or rather, this certain interest or attention already shows the beginning of an accord with the hostile will. For evil always presupposes freedom; otherwise, it would be merely coercion, conquering man from without.

Man sinned freely. So then, what was the original sin?

[28] *The Revelations of St. Seraphim of Sarov* (Paris, 1932).

[29] The passage where the three wills are mentioned is to be found in Letter 20, published in Galland, *Veterum Patrum Bibliotheca* (Venice, 1788) vol. IV, 696 and ff.

[30] For the detailed analysis of these terms see V. Zarine, *The Foundations of Orthodox Asceticism* (St. Petersburg, 1902). This text is still valuable.

[31] "On Baptism," P.G. 65, col. 1020A.

[32] St. Mark the Hermit, "On Spiritual Law," 142, P.G. 65, col. 921-924.

The Fathers of the Church distinguished several moments in the determining of free will, which separates man from God. The moral moment (and that means the personal moment) is contained, in the opinion of all the Fathers, in disobedience to, violation of, the divine plan. If man had accepted God's commandment in the spirit of filial love, he would have responded to God's will in complete self-renunciation, he would willingly have rejected not only the forbidden fruit, but also every external object, so as to live only in God, to strive single-mindedly for union with Him. God's commandment showed human will the path to follow to attain deification, the path of the renunciation of all that is not God. But human will chose the opposite path. Separating itself from God, it submitted itself to the power of the devil. St. Gregory of Nyssa and St. Maximus the Confessor have turned their attention particularly to the physical side of sin: instead of following its natural disposition towards God, the human mind turned towards the world; instead of spiritualizing the body, it gave itself to the current of animal and sensual life, submitted itself to the material world. St. Simeon the New Theologian[33] sees the progressive development of sin in the fact that man, instead of repenting, attempts to justify himself before God: Adam lays the entire responsibility on Eve, "the wife that Thou gavest me," thus making God the original cause of his own fall. Eve accuses the serpent. Refusing to recognize that the origin of evil exists solely in their own free will, men reject the possibility of freeing themselves from evil, and submit their freedom to external necessity. The will hardens and closes itself against God. As Philaret, Metropolitan of Moscow, says, "Man has arrested in himself the effluence of divine grace."

Did the very loss of grace occasion man's fall into sin? The notion of *gratia supererogatoria*, that is, grace which is added to nature in order to direct it towards God, is foreign to the teaching of the Eastern Church. Made in God's image, the human person was directed to its prototype, its

[33]The Forty-fifth Oration in the Smyrna edition and in Russian translation. The Thirty-third Oration in the Latin translation, ed. Migne, P.G. 120, col. 449AB.

nature irresistibly sought God by virtue of its will, which is a spiritual and rational power. "The righteousness of primitive man" was based on the fact that man, having been made by God, could only be a good nature, directed to good, that is, to communion with God, to the acquisition of uncreated grace. If this good nature strayed from its creator, it could only have happened through its capacity for inner self-determination, its αὐτεξουσία. It is this that gives man the possibility of acting and willing not only in conformity with his natural inclinations, but also in opposition to his own nature, which he can distort and make "anti-nature."

The fall of human nature is the direct consequence of the free self-determination of man, who voluntarily subjected himself to this condition. The anti-natural condition must lead to the disintegration of human nature; this disintegration finds its conclusion in death, which is the final stage in distorted nature's falling away from God. In this distorted nature there is no longer any place for uncreated grace; in it, according to St. Gregory of Nyssa, the mind, like the obverse of a mirror, instead of reflecting God, takes into itself the image of formless matter,[34] where the passions violate the original hierarchical structure of the human being. The loss of grace is not therefore the cause, but rather the consequence of the fall into sin. Man has obstructed in himself the capacity for communion with God, has closed the path of grace, which should have poured through him onto all of creation.

This physical interpretation of sin and its consequences does not exclude, in the teaching of the Eastern Church, the other side, which always imposes itself: the personal, moral aspect of sin, that is, transgression and punishment. The two aspects are inseparably bound together, because man is not only a nature, but also a person confronting a personal God, in a personal relationship with Him. If human nature disintegrates as a consequence of sin, if sin introduces death into the created world, then this is not only because human nature has created a new condition (ἕξις), a new mode of

[34]*On the Structure of Man*, XII, P.G. 44, col. 164.

existence in evil, but also because God has set a limit to sin, allowing it to end in death: "For the wages (*stipendia*, ὀψώνια) of sin is death." "We are offspring of a tarnished race,"[35] said St. Macarius of Egypt. However, nothing in nature, not even the demons, is essentially evil.

But sin, this parasite of nature, having taken root in the will, becomes a kind of "anti-grace." It penetrates into being, living in it, making it the devil's prisoner. The devil is himself the prisoner of his own will, perpetually fixed in evil. There appears in the world a new pole, opposite to the image of God. This pole, illusory in itself, becomes real through the will (such is the paradox of its possessing being in very non-being, of which St. Gregory of Nyssa speaks). Through human will, evil becomes a power which infects creation ("accursed is the earth for thy sake," says Genesis). The cosmos, which eternally reflects divine majesty, simultaneously acquires a sinister aspect, "the noctural aspect of creation," in the words of one Russian theologian and philosopher. Sin is introduced where grace should have reigned, and instead of divine plenitude, a yawning abyss of non-being is opened in God's creation: the gates of Hell are opened by man's free will.

Adam did not fulfill his vocation. He knew neither how to attain union with God nor how to deify the created world. That which he did not accomplish when he enjoyed the fullness of his freedom became for him impossible from the moment that he voluntarily enslaved himself to an external power. From the Fall until the day of Pentecost, divine energy, uncreated and deifying grace, remained foreign to human nature and acted upon it only from outside. The prophets and the righteous men of the Old Testament were instruments of grace. Grace acted through their mediation, but was not imparted to men as their personal power. Deification, union with God through grace, had become impossible. But the divine plan was not destroyed by human sin: the vocation of the first Adam was fulfilled by Christ,

[35]On the dark powers invading the human spirit, see *Spiritual Homilies* XXIV, 2, XLIII, 7-9 and P.G. 34, col. 664, 776-777. Russian translation of the *Works* of St. Macarius of Egypt, pp. 181-182, 280-281.

the second Adam. In the words of St. Irenaeus of Lyon and St. Athanasius the Great, repeated by the holy Fathers and theologians of every age, "God became man in order that man might become God."[36] However, this work, completed by the Incarnate Word, appears to fallen mankind in its most immediate aspect, as the work of salvation, the redemption of a world enslaved by sin and death. Those who are tempted by the teaching of the *felix culpa* often forget that, in destroying the domination of sin, our Saviour opened to us anew the way to deification, which is the ultimate end of man. Thus the work of Christ brings with it the work of the Holy Spirit (Luke 12:49).

[36]St. Irenaeus of Lyon, *Against Heresies*, V, preface, P.G. 7, col. 1120; St. Athanasius the Great, "Oration on the Incarnation of the Word of God," 54, P.G. 25, col. 192B; St. Gregory of Nazianzus, *Poëm. Dogmatica*, X, 5-9, P.G. 37, col. 465; St. Gregory of Nyssa, "The Great Catechetical Oration," 25, P.G. 45, col. 65D.